Northern Irish Images

Cornelsen

Northern Irish Images

Herausgegeben von
Sheila McBride-Gutknecht, Erlangen
Valerie McCord-Hellmann, Erlangen
Hilary Reid, Nürnberg

Verlagsredaktion
Dr. Christian v. Raumer

Beratende Mitwirkung
Máire Tully-Napier, Lisburn

Technische Umsetzung
Lutz Hagemoser

Text- und Bildquellen vgl. S. 79
Umschlagfotos: Britain on View – BTA/ETB (oben); Stuart Franklin/Magnum (unten)

1. Auflage 1990
Alle Drucke dieser Auflage können, weil untereinander unverändert,
im Unterricht nebeneinander verwendet werden.

Druck: Adolph Fürst & Sohn, Berlin

ISBN 3-464-05212-5
Vertrieb: Cornelsen Verlagsgesellschaft, Bielefeld
Bestellnummer: 52125

Contents

Abbreviations and symbols

abbr.	abbreviation
adj.	adjective
adv.	adverb
AE	mainly or exclusively American English
BE	mainly or exclusively British English
C	countable noun
cf.	confer; compare (with); see
Co.	County
derog.	derogatory
e.g.	exempli gratia; for example
esp.	especially
fig.	figurative(ly)
fml.	formal
Fr.	French
i.e.	id est; that is
infml.	informal
interj.	interjection
Ital.	Italian
l./ll.	line, lines
lang.	language
lit.	literary
n.	noun
N.I.	Northern Irish; Northern Ireland
p./pp.	page, pages
pl.	plural
pron.	pronunciation
sb.	somebody
Scot.	Scottish
sl.	slang
sth.	something
U	uncountable noun
usu.	usually
v.	verb
vulg.	vulgar

☆ American pronunciation follows

Chapter I

Northern Ireland – A Tourist Attraction?

1

Cal McCrystal

An Untamed Land So Far from Trouble

Although Northern Ireland is frequently in the news, it is not a place many people visit. This neglect is undeserved, as the author of the following article from *The Sunday Times* argues.

There is a corner in Europe, little visited by the masses, which attracts every summer a select and devoted *cognoscenti*. It is not much more than 5,000 square miles in size and of indifferent climate. Visitors may have difficulty with its language and its traditions. Yet, year after year without fail, the *cognoscenti* return to fish its beautiful lakes, sail its long estuaries, pace its deserted beaches, penetrate its ferny woods or wander its briary roads.

They see a chameleon landscape: black basalt rock melting into impossibly-green pasture; hill-tops shattered by nature into fantastical shapes; tiny fields with the undulations of a basket of eggs; desolate moorland.

After a few days there, 120 years ago, William Makepeace Thackeray wrote of part of it: "It looks like the beginning of the world, somehow: the sea looks older than in other places, the hills and rocks strange, and formed differently from other rocks and hills – as those vast dubious monsters were formed who possessed the earth before man ... When the world was moulded and fashioned out of formless chaos, this must have been the bit over – a remnant of chaos!"

The *cognoscenti* who go there today will stumble across squat, enigmatical stone figures, resembling those from the Iberian bronze age and suggesting pagan worship and ritual; a town named after the surrounding Sacred Plain; a city named after a queen who lived 2,300 years ago; 6th century Christian monasteries; and 20th century Christian practices which include the painting of kerb-stones to hem in the past and the beating of drums far into the night to bash the future into submission.

The natives (1.5m of them) maintain an unyielding high opinion of this territory. Yet they sometimes evince surprise that the foreigner should share their enthusiasms. Hence the effusiveness of their greeting and the overwhelming hospitality that cushions the visitor from sudden dissonance.

This, you see, is Ulster – the battered province, the Red Handland of mangled cities, riotous assembly and sustained terror. A holiday resort? Surely not!

A tourist attraction on the north coast of Northern Ireland: Giant's Causeway

But yes, they do go there: Germans, Spanish, Dutch, Scandinavians, North Americans, quite a few British. The *cognoscenti* total only about 130,000 but they are increasing steadily year by year, provoking some obvious questions:

Aren't they scared? No. They head for the bits that are not mangled, riotous or terrorised.

But aren't these bits hard to find? Not at all. They constitute most of the territory. Tourists leave after two weeks of wholesome sport, food and friendship without hearing an angry word or stubbing a toe on a half-brick.

Yeah, but what about the towns? What's a holiday without night-life? Belfast, the capital, has good theatres and lots of ethnic restaurants along a strip nick-named The Golden Mile. Some of it is a bit flaky. There is little to enchant here. Stick to the wonderful coast and the hinterland, where night-life is safer, less pretentious and more rewarding.

The language ... isn't that a problem? You soon get used to it with the help of published language courses from the remarkable author, John Pepper.

Jinnomabror? means, do you know my brother? *Blaka ribbel* – a block of ripple ice-cream. *Biasabunma* means, buy me a bun, mother! *Naawalnat* means, no, I will not.

Failing that, you can escape to solitary places where no human chatter interrupts the sounds which one ought to associate with the province: the cries of sea birds on the rocky Antrim cliffs, the whoosh of waves against the great dark headlands and the murmuring reeds of Fermanagh lakeland.

And there are even remoter solitudes – the Sperrins, with the bewitching forests of Seskinore and Pomeroy and inexpensive guns for pheasant, woodcock, pigeon, hare and rabbit; the central area of the Mournes, known as The Wilderness; Rathlin Island, six miles off the north coast where 20,000 guillemots, razorbills, shearwaters, fulmars, kittiwakes and puffins exist comfortably with 30 hardy human families.

There is no hint here of what keeps so many people away.

Tourism in Northern Ireland has been a nightmare for its organisers during the past 17 years since the start of what the tourist board calls the "civil disturbances". Costly advertising campaigns were countered by terrorist explosions, sectarian warfare, violent intimidation – all seen on TV screens in Europe and America.

But the unrest has failed to daunt significant numbers of visiting friends and relatives (approximately 455,000), or of businessmen (191,000), or shoppers from the Irish Republic (70,000), all of whom visit the province in ever-increasing numbers. Understandably, it has blocked the arrival of hundreds of thousands of ordinary tourists.

It does not deter the "war groupies", mostly young Dutch and West German travellers for whom no holiday is a success without elements of danger. You may catch glimpses of them in Beirut or in Central America, trying to look like hard-boiled war correspondents, looking forward to developing those happy snaps with the barbed-wire background and charging their batteries on other people's atrocities and miseries.

But they are not to be confused with the *cognoscenti.* "I take a boat here almost every year," says one of them from Hamburg as he ties up his rented cabin-cruiser at one of Lough Erne's many small marinas. He has come with friends to take bream, pike, gudgeon and trout and to further explore the 154 islands and innumerable channels of Fermanagh's lakeland.

"My family has been here and they love it. We hope to be back next year. To me the advantage is not just the beauty of the place; it's that not many people come here to spoil it. That is ironic, isn't it? It's a little bit terrible to say so, but the fears of the many have provided us with a placid vacation."

One sees what he means as one drives north of Belfast, along the sensational Antrim coast road to sheltered little bays like Cushendall where good, cheap hotel accommodation can be found, and Whitepark where the road runs high above a golden strand and the rollers run white and clean; to tiny Bushmills where heaven matures in ancient casks; to the Giant's Causeway, Thackeray's "remnant of chaos".

It is a good idea to continue westwards through Londonderry (one of the loveliest-sited cities in Europe) into Donegal – in the Irish Republic, but part of historic Ulster – then south to Belleek, just back over the border, where exquisite china is made. One is now at the western tip of Lower Lough Erne and in one of the most enchanting lakelands of the world. Far from The Troubles, one feels oneself a privileged member of the *cognoscenti.*

3 *cognoscente* (pl. *cognoscenti*) [ˌkɒnjə'ʃentɪ ☆ -tiː] (Ital.): Kenner/in **5** *indifferent:* neither very good nor very bad; second-rate **9** *estuary* ['estʃʊərɪ ☆ -ʊeriː]: wide river mouth **11** *briary:* full of or flanked by thorny bushes **16** *undulation:* wave-like slope; hill **19** *William Makepeace Thackeray* (1811–1863): English novelist **29** *remnant:* small remaining part; surviving trace **31** *enigmatical:* mysterious **34–35** *a town named after the surrounding Sacred Plain:* reference to Omagh ['əʊmə] **35–36** *a city named after a queen:* reference to Armagh [ɑː'mɑː], which is named after the Irish Queen Macha ['mæxə] **39** *the painting of kerb-stones:* reference to the Northern Irish Protestant practice of painting the edge of a pavement red, white and blue (i.e. the colours of the British flag) **39–40** *hem in sb./sth.:* restrict sb./sth. **40** *the beating of drums:* reference to the Northern Irish Protestant practice of beating large drums around the 12th July to commemorate the Battle of the Boyne (cf. "Info-Box", p. 21) **44** *unyielding* (adj.): firm **45** *evince sth.* (fml.): show, exhibit sth. (a feeling or a quality) **47** *effusiveness:* quality of showing (too much) feeling **52** *Red Handland:* reference to the badge of Northern Ireland, which shows an upright red hand (cf. photograph, p. 74) • *mangle sb./sth.:* mutilate sb., damage sth. greatly **53** *sustain sb./sth.:* keep sb./sth. in existence **66–67** *wholesome:* good for one's health **75** *flaky:* (here) showing signs of old age • *enchant sb.*[–ˈ–]: fill sb. with great delight **82** *John Pepper:* cf. Ch. III, Text 3 **92** *Antrim:* county in Northern Ireland **94** *Fermanagh* [fə'mænə]: county in Northern Ireland **103–105** *guillemots* ['gɪlɪmɒts], *razorbills, shearwaters, fulmars, kittiwakes and puffins:* types of sea-birds **118** *daunt sb.* [dɔːnt]: discourage, frighten sb. **127** *deter sb.* [dɪ'tɜː ☆ -'tɜːr]: discourage, frighten sb. **144** *bream, pike, gudgeon* ['gʌdʒən] *and trout:* types of freshwater-fish **154** *placid* ['plæsɪd]: calm, peaceful **163** *Bushmills:* small town with a famous whiskey distillery

Fermanagh lakeland

Talking about the text

1. According to the article, what are the reasons for the relative lack of tourism in Northern Ireland?
2. What type of people visit Ulster and what are their reasons for travelling there?
3. How does the author characterize the Northern Irish?
4. What is the author's attitude to the promotion of tourism in Northern Ireland and why could it be said to be ambiguous?

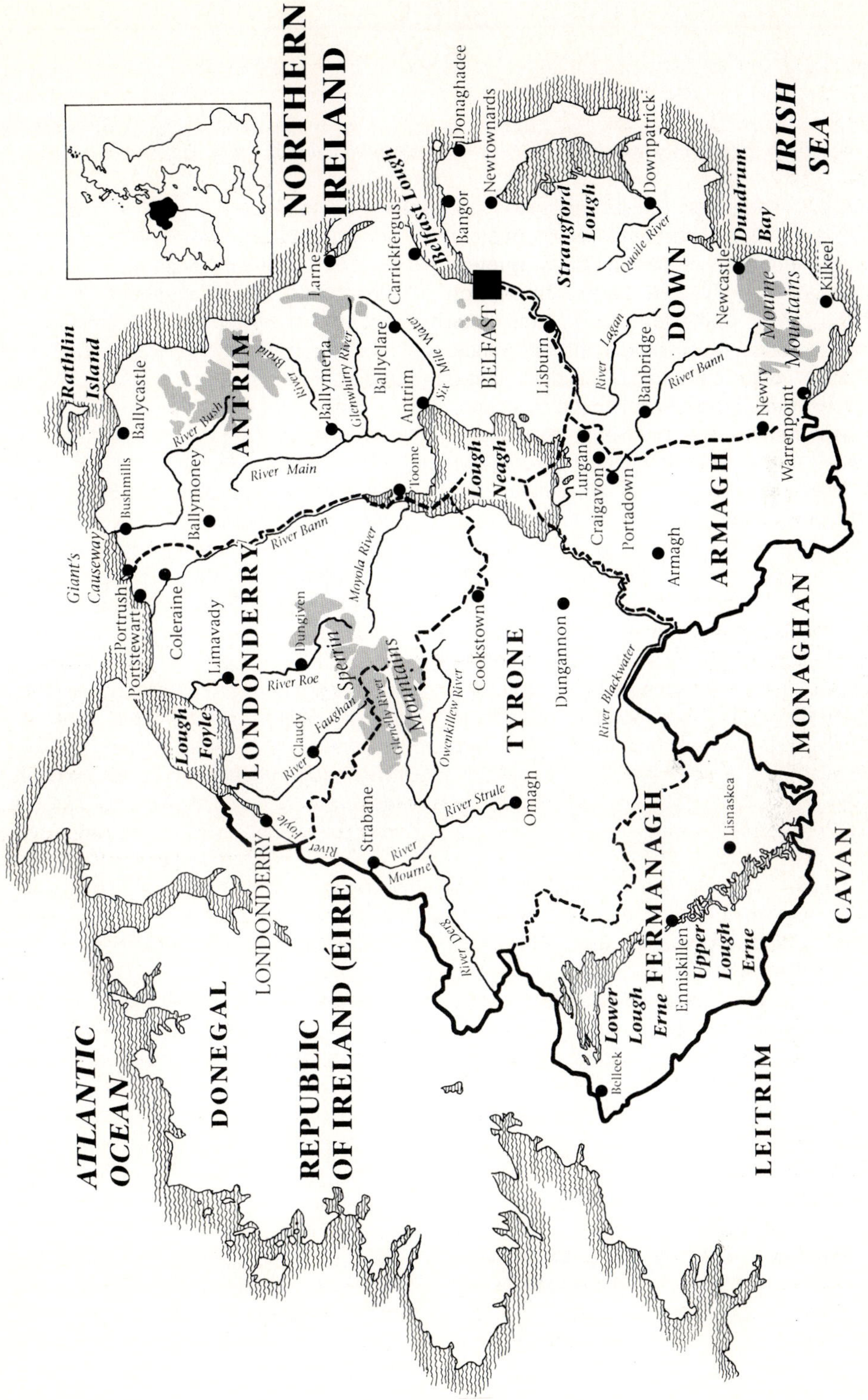
NORTHERN IRELAND
ATLANTIC OCEAN
IRISH SEA
REPUBLIC OF IRELAND (ÉIRE)
DONEGAL
LEITRIM
CAVAN
MONAGHAN
ANTRIM
LONDONDERRY
TYRONE
FERMANAGH
ARMAGH
DOWN
Rathlin Island
Giant's Causeway
Ballycastle
Bushmills
Portrush
Portstewart
Coleraine
Ballymoney
Limavady
Dungiven
Claudy
LONDONDERRY
Strabane
Omagh
Cookstown
Dungannon
Toome
Ballymena
Antrim
Ballyclare
Larne
Carrickfergus
Bangor
Donaghadee
Newtownards
BELFAST
Lisburn
Lurgan
Craigavon
Portadown
Armagh
Banbridge
Newry
Warrenpoint
Newcastle
Kilkeel
Downpatrick
Enniskillen
Lisnaskea
Belleek
Lough Foyle
Lough Neagh
Belfast Lough
Strangford Lough
Dundrum Bay
Lower Lough Erne
Upper Lough Erne
Sperrin Mountains
Mourne Mountains
River Bush
River Main
River Bann
River Braid
Glenwhirry River
Six Mile Water
River Lagan
Quoile River
River Roe
River Faughan
River Foyle
Moyola River
Glenelly River
Owenkillew River
River Strule
River Mourne
River Derg
River Blackwater

INFO BOX

Northern Ireland in a Nutshell

Natural features: On its northern and eastern sides, Northern Ireland has an indented coastline of cliffs and bays with Lough Foyle, Belfast Lough, Strangford Lough and Carlingford Lough being the largest indentations.The landscape varies and is made up of some of the oldest rocks in the British Isles, basalt in the north east and granite in the south-east, resulting in the three main mountainous regions, the Antrim Plateau in the north-east, the Mourne Mountains in the south-east and the Sperrin Mountains in the north-west of the province. The highest peak is Slieve Donard (852 m) in the Mourne Mountains.

Lough Neagh, in the centre of Northern Ireland, is the largest inland lake in the British Isles, measuring 381 sq km. In the south-west of the province one finds a large lake system, comprising Upper and Lower Lough Erne.

Size: 13,567 sq km

Climate: The climate is mild, the Gulf Stream flowing along the west coast of Ireland ensuring that the temperature seldom falls below freezing point in winter. The average annual rainfall is 108 cm. The average winter temperature is between 4° and 7°C, the average summer temperature is between 14° and 16°C, although it may rise to 25 °C between June and August.

Population: 1,575,200 (1987)

Density of population: 117 inhabitants per sq km (cf. England: 364 inhabitants per sq km)

Religious denominations (1981):

Roman Catholic		28.0 %
Protestant	Presbyterian	22.9 %
	Church of Ireland	19.0 %
	Methodist	4.0 %
Other		7.6 %
No information		18.5 %

The figures are based on the 1981 census. At the time, a large number of people in Northern Ireland refused to give any information about their religion. It is estimated that Protestants outnumber Catholics by roughly 2 to 1.

Major cities: Belfast (population 303,800) is the capital of Northern Ireland. Londonderry (or Derry, as it is also known), with 97,500 inhabitants, is the second largest city. Newtownabbey, with 72,300 people, is officially third in population but is, in fact, a northern suburb of Belfast. The New Town of Craigavon (population 76,600) was formed in 1965 by joining the towns of Lurgan and Portadown.

Economy: Over 100,000 people are engaged in agriculture (farming or food production). Historically, most industrial development took place in the east of Northern Ireland, with Belfast as a centre of the linen, ship-building, aircraft and engineering industries. While the textile and ship-building industries have declined, aircraft-building is still important. Today there are many smaller manufacturing businesses in Northern Ireland, and tourism is gaining in importance (1.1 million visitors in 1989). Nevertheless, the unemployment rate was 16.7% in 1988.

Administration: From 1921 to 1972 Northern Ireland was a partly self-governing province of the United Kingdom with a regional parliament at Stormont. Since 1972 it has been under direct rule from Westminster, with its own Secretary of State.

Northern Ireland is also known by various other names:

- *Ulster:* This was the name of one of the ancient Celtic provinces of Ireland, the other three being Munster, Leinster and Connacht. Although commonly used as a synonym for Northern Ireland, the term is slightly incorrect: historically Ulster consisted not of six, but of nine counties, three of which are now part of the Republic of Ireland.
- *The province:* i.e.the province of Ulster.
- *The six counties:* The term is normally used by residents of the Republic of Ireland only. Northern Ireland consists of the counties Antrim, Armagh, Down, Fermanagh, Londonderry (also called Derry) and Tyrone. (Similarly, the Republic of Ireland is sometimes referred to as "the 26 counties".)
- *The North:* Often used by residents of the Republic of Ireland.

The first two terms are favoured by Protestants, the last two by Catholics, although all four terms may be used by either.

2

Alf McCreary

Belfast – Charming and Exasperating

In his book *An Ulster Journey* (1986) Alf McCreary takes a look at the people and places of Northern Ireland from a traveller's point of view. In the following excerpt the author portrays the city of Belfast.

This jewel that houses our hopes and our fears
Was knocked up from the swamp in the last hundred years;
But the last shall be first and the first shall be last;
May the Lord in His mercy be kind to Belfast...

O the bricks they will bleed and the rain it will weep,
And the damp Lagan fog lull the city to sleep;
It's to hell with the future and live on the past;
May the Lord in His mercy be kind to Belfast.

These words of Maurice James Craig in the second and last verses of his "Ballad to a Traditional Refrain" summarise a common kind of despair about this tough, maddening and yet charming city which enjoys one of the most beautiful settings in the world. It lies at the centre of a hollow of green hills, with the long, blue ribbon of Belfast Lough stretching from the Irish Sea to its very heart.

The cross-channel ferries glide almost to the pavements of inner Belfast. At Custom House Square the red and cream corporation buses and the busy traffic move past the huge up-turned bow of the Isle of Man steamer as it disgorges its cargo. The gleaming white superstructure and the dark hull are almost unnoticed, as if this visitor is as much a fixture of Belfast as the elegant Custom House of Charles Lanyon, which is one of the city's architectural jewels. People hurry past in their mechanical boxes, with hardly a glance at ship, quay or architecture. The magnificent sculpture of Neptune, Britannia and Mercury on the seaward side of the Custom House, is now guarded by a wire grill high on the building, as if the city's considerable sea-going history is now being symbolically barred from public view. Most people hardly notice it anymore.

Belfast is a city which takes itself and its history for granted. As a major port on the island, the heart of Belfast's history has been the sea, and the people of Belfast have been like the ocean itself – sometimes wild and whipped-up, then quiet and re-assuring in the

"Jewel" or "awful city"? Belfast with the City Hall

ebb of storm, or exhilarating with a sharp freshness that sweeps to excitement, or grey and menacing. But always there is a surge of raw energy which makes Belfast so vibrant and so unpredictably charming, and at times utterly exasperating.

The Lord in His mercy may indeed be kind to Belfast, as Maurice James Craig implores, but most mortals – and writers – are not. The descriptive vitriol of Ulsterman Brian Moore, describing the area around the City Hall, has lasted as long as his novel *The Lonely Passion of Judith Hearne*. "There, under the great dome of the building, ringed around by forgotten memorials, bordered by the garrison neatness of a Garden of Remembrance, everything that was Belfast came into focus. The newsvendors calling out the great events of the world in flat, uninterested Ulster voices; the drab facades of the buildings grouped around the Square, proclaiming the virtues of trade, hard dealing and Presbyterian righteousness.

"The order, the neatness, the floodlit cenotaph, a white respectable phallus planted in sinking Irish bog. The Protestant dearth of gaiety, the Protestant surfeit of order, the dour Ulster burghers walking proudly among these monuments to their mediocrity."

Nearly 30 years later an American writer, Paul Theroux, was only a little less acerbic. "I knew at once that Belfast was an awful city. It had a bad face – mouldering buildings, tough-looking people, a visible smell, too many fences ... It was so awful I wanted to stay ... I lingered a few days marvelling at its decrepitude and then vowed to come back the following week. I had never seen anything like it. ..."

The Dublin-based actor, wit and writer Micheál Mac Liammóir once observed: "Belfast is the capital of the Six Counties and its people are not by any means invariably harsh, pragmatical, cold, bigoted or rude; nor are the majority of the people of Derry, Tyrone, Armagh or any of the other Northern counties I know. Some of them, of course, have all these distressing qualities, but the same thing could be said of many people in other places. Even in Italy, even in Greece, even in Southern Ireland, one meets them here and there."

He was both eloquent and perceptive about Belfast and its people. "There are poets and painters who live in this oddly ugly city that has for me a peculiar charm of its own. Perhaps it is the charm of disguise, for that is one of the first things you notice about it: it wears a mask. Everything possible is done to hide up the fact that you are in Ireland at all: the Irish language is seldom heard and never seen ... 'Ulster is British!' is the motto everywhere, and but for the blue mountains at the end of the streets, the quality of the light, the sigh of the wind, certain faces and voices, certain hints of melancholy and of magic lightly touching you as day passes into night, you might easily believe yourself to be in Bradford or Manchester."

2 *knock sth. up:* construct sth. hurriedly **6** *Lagan* ['lægən]: river flowing through Belfast • *lull sb./sth.:* make sb./sth. (a person or an animal) quiet; soothe sb./sth. **9** *Maurice James Craig* (1919–): Belfast writer and poet **15** *corporation:* (in Britain) city council **16** *bow* [baʊ]: front end of a boat or ship • *disgorge sth.* [–'–]: throw out sth. (e.g. food) from the stomach or throat; (here) unload sth. **17** *hull:* body of a ship **18** *fixture* (infml.): person or thing that is firmly established • *Charles Lanyon* (1813–1889): British architect **27** *exhilarating* (adj.): very exciting; causing happiness **28** *menace sb./sth.* ['– –]: threaten sb./sth. • *surge* (n.): sudden occurence or increase **30** *implore:* beg earnestly **31** *vitriol* (fig.): sarcastic comment **31–32** *Brian Moore* (1921–): Irish-born novelist who has lived in Canada and the USA since 1948 **34** *Garden of Remembrance:* garden to commemorate those killed in the two world war **38** *Presbyterian* (adj.): of or belonging to the Presbyterian Church (cf. "Info-Box", p. 10) • *righteousness:* (U): quality of wanting to do what is morally right **39** *cenotaph* ['senətɑːf ☆ -tæf]: monument in memory of people buried elsewhere, esp. soldiers killed in war **40** *dearth* [dɜːθ ☆ dɜːrθ]: shortage, lack • *surfeit* ['sɜːfɪt ☆ 'sɜːr-]: too much of something, excess • *dour* [dʊə ☆ dʊər]: stern, humourless **41** *mediocrity:* quality of being neither very good nor very bad **42** *Paul Theroux* [θə'ruː] (1941–): US author now living in London • *acerbic* [ə'sɜːbɪk ☆ -'sɜːr-] (fml.): harsh, bitter **43** *moulder* (BE) = (AE) *molder* (v.): crumble to dust by natural decay **45** *linger* ['lɪŋgə ☆ -gər] (v.): stay for a long time;

be unwilling to leave • *decrepitude* (U): state of being weak by age **47** *wit:* clever and amusing person • *Micheál Mac Liammóir* ['mɪhɔːl mək'lɪəmɔː] (1899–1978): Irish actor, playwright and theatre director **48** *Six Counties* (infml.): Northern Ireland **49** *bigoted* ['bɪgətɪd] (adj.): intolerant and narrow-minded • *Tyrone* [tɪ'rəʊn] **50** *Armagh* [ɑː'mɑː]

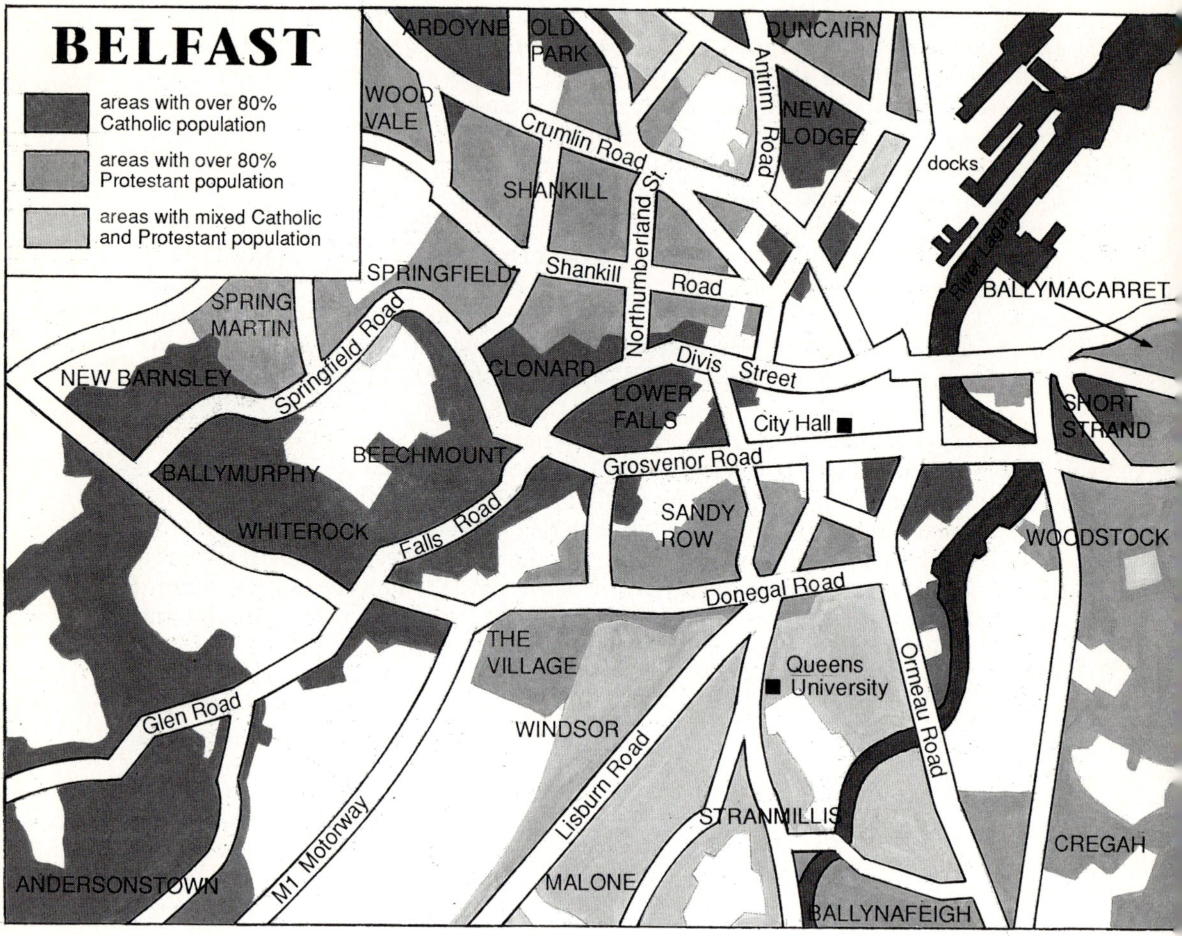

Talking about the text

1. Give a description of Belfast's geographical location, referring to the text and the map of Northern Ireland on p. 9.
2. Explain the importance Belfast's location had for the city's development.
3. What were Brian Moore's and Paul Theroux's impressions of Belfast?
4. According to the writers quoted in the text, what are some of the main characteristics of the people of Belfast?
5. Explain what is meant by the term "disguise" in l. 56 .

3

DERVLA MURPHY
A Journey of Courage

In the foreword to her book about Northern Ireland the Southern Irish writer and traveller Dervla Murphy explains her reasons for finally visiting a country which up till then had not interested her in the least.

Before June 1976 I had spent in Northern Ireland precisely thirty-six hours out of forty-four years. My one crossing of the border, in September 1973, was to give a talk in Enniskillen; and as soon as possible I was on my way home having felt no urge to stand and stare. To me, in County Waterford, Northern Ireland was merely a squalid little briar-patch swarming with human anachronisms – who often seemed sub-human – and seething with dreary dissensions punctuated by ghastly excesses. Since there seemed to be nothing anybody could do about it, it was best forgotten. So I went to South India that winter, and to Baltistan the following winter, and wherever I went people asked me why Christians were fighting in Ireland. To which I replied impatiently that I didn't know myself. It never occurred to me that this reply, from an Irishwoman, betrayed an attitude both stupid and unkind; even, some might say, irresponsible.

In the Spring of 1976, after listening to two of the more bone-headed Northern politicians arguing on the wireless one evening, I was appalled to hear myself saying viciously, "Why don't the Brits get out and let them slaughter each other if that's how they feel? There's nothing to choose between them. Why did we ever long for a united Ireland?" It was then that this book was conceived, by shame out of repentance. It is not a study of history, politics, theology, geography, sociology, economics or guerrilla warfare. It is simply an honest portrayal of emotions – my own and other people's – and an attempt to find the sources of those emotions. At one stage I had hoped to be able to clarify the present Northern Irish turmoil for the ordinary citizens of Britain and the Republic. But the more time I spent up North the less capable I felt doing any such thing.

In Ireland, during recent years, many Southerners have been voicing anti-Northern sentiments with increasing vehemence and frequency. Some such outbursts may be excused on the grounds of frustration and despair but most, I fear, are symptoms of a spreading infection. To me it seems unlikely that the North's physical violence will ever overflow seriously into the South, yet this is a tiny island and gradually the emotional violence "up there" has affected the atmosphere "down here". Moreover, because the Provisional IRA hope one day to be free to transfer their attentions to the Republic, many – less optimistic than myself – feel threatened by the Northern chaos. And the maggots of bigotry breed so fast on fear that we may soon see a new form of intolerance in Ireland, between Southern and Northern Catholics.

It is ironical (or do I mean comical?) that so many in the Republic are so thankful now that Westminster rather than Dublin is responsible for Northern Ireland. And it seems odd that, despite decades of political bombast and emotional white-heats about a united Ireland, so few of us have ever crossed the border or taken a normal neighbourly interest in our Northern fellow-countrymen. It is true, sadly, that there is nothing tangible we in the South could do. But the intangible also counts. Why should we not travel in the North to express a concerned interest in the people there and see for ourselves what really goes on, as distinct from what the media choose to tell us? When I urge my friends to holiday in Northern Ireland they look at me as though I were delirious. Yet it is an entirely sensible suggestion, from every point of view. Visitors from the South would find books, beer and butter cheaper than at home. And they would find the people as welcoming, the scenery as good, the roads better and the weather no worse.

Breathtaking view: Glenariff, County Antrim, opening onto the Irish Sea

Having cycled hundreds of miles through superb countryside, and into (and safely out of) dozens of small towns and villages, I feel no hesitation about recommending the rural North of Ireland as a holiday area for families of any nationality. During July and August I was accompanied by my seven-year-old daughter, Rachel, who rode her pony, Scamp, for more than 300 miles while I cycled ahead and her elkhound, Olaf, trotted along behind. We camped out in a tiny tent in the counties of Fermanagh, Tyrone, Londonderry and Donegal and spent a night in a field bisected by the border. While we slept in Northern Ireland Scamp grazed in the Republic. It was not a bit like what you read in the papers.

However, these were not my sentiments as I cycled North in early June from my tranquil home in the far South. I then experienced, at intervals, sick little spasms of fear. Even those of us who cherish our independence of thought can no longer protect our emotions from the influence of the media; though we may continue to think for ourselves, our feelings are all the time being manipulated. Also, for weeks my local friends (perfectly sensible people, most of them) had been begging me to "forget Ulster" – which naturally increased both my determination to go and my nervousness. Never before had I embarked on a journey that required courage.

3 *urge* [ɜːdʒ ☆ ɜːrdʒ]: desire **4** *County Waterford:* county in the south of the Republic of Ireland • *squalid* ['skwɒlɪd ☆ 'skwɑː-]: dirty and neglected **4–5** *briar-patch:* small area with thorny hedges **5** *swarm with sb./sth.:* be full of sb./sth. **6** *seethe with sth.:* be very agitated and full of sth. • *dreary:* dull, boring • *dissension:* disagreement in opinion • *punctuate sth.:* interrupt sth. at intervals **8** *Baltistan:* region in Kashmir **13** *appal sb.* [ə'pɔːl]: fill sb. with fear or terror **14** *Brits* (derog.): British armed forces in Northern Ireland **16** *repentance* (U): regret **20** *turmoil* ['tɜːmɔɪl ☆ 'tɜːr-]: agitation, confusion **28** *Provisional IRA* (abbr.) = *Provisional Irish Republican Army:* militant organization of Irish nationalists (cf. "Info-Box", p. 23) **29** *maggot:* Made **30** *bigotry* (U): stubborn intolerance, narrowmindedness **34** *white-heat* ['– –] (fig.): great enthusiasm **36** *tangible* ['tændʒəbl]: concrete, definite **48** *elkhound:* large Norwegian dog **49–50** *Fermanagh* [fə'mænə], *Tyrone* [tɪ'rəʊn], *Londonderry:* counties in Northern Ireland **50** *Donegal* [ˌdʌnɪ'gɔːl]: northernmost county of the Republic of Ireland **54** *spasm* ['spæzəm]: sudden and uncontrollable tightening of one's muscles **55** *cherish sb./sth.:* love sb./sth. **60** *embark on sth.:* start sth.

Talking about the text

1. Describe Dervla Murphy's change of attitude in the seventies to Northern Ireland and its problems.
2. What were her motives for writing the book to which this text is an introduction?
3. How does the writer explain the increase of anti-northern sentiments in the Republic of Ireland?
4. Why does she think Northern Ireland is a good holiday area both for Southerners and people of other nationalities?
5. How would you explain Murphy's statement that she had never before "embarked on a journey that required courage" (l. 60)?

Chapter II

Civil Unrest

1

Edmund Curran, Frederick Painton

Twenty Years on, "When Will It Ever End?"

20 years after the conflict began in 1968, the authors of the following article from an American news magazine ask why violence continues in Northern Ireland in spite of widespread disapproval in both the Protestant and Roman Catholic communities.

In other parts of the world, it was an exceptionally good week for peace. Iran and Iraq agreed to a cease-fire; South Africa, Angola and Cuba announced a cessation of hostilities in southwestern Africa. The Soviets are finishing the first phase of a troop pullout from Afghanistan.

In one of the longest and in some ways cruelest of contemporary conflicts, however, the killing goes on – if on a much smaller scale. The British province of Ulster will not stop to mark a grim anniversary this month, the 20th year of a terrorist conflict involving a Protestant majority and Roman Catholic minority, with the British army caught in the middle. For a long time now, the ancient grievances that first triggered the clash between the two communities have appeared largely irrelevant, but the confrontation keeps refueling itself in a deadly, mindless cycle of attack and revenge.

And so Belfast's Roman Catholic Bishop Cahal Daly made yet another impassioned plea for peace last week. "The community and specifically the Catholic community are weary of the 20-year-old sorrow," declared the bishop. "They are asking, 'When will it ever end?'" The occasion was despairingly familiar: a Requiem Mass for another victim of the violence. Held in West Belfast's St. Agnes Church, the service mourned Peter Dolan, 25, a truck driver's assistant. Dolan, along with Seamus Morris, 18, a student, was gunned down in the poor, Catholic Ardoyne district of Belfast by a hit team riding in a stolen car. The Protestant Action Force, a paramilitary group, claimed responsibility and said the shooting was in retaliation for an ambush by the outlawed Irish Republican Army the previous week in which two elderly Protestant men died. "For the love of God," implored Bishop Daly at the service. "For the love of Ireland, and for the sake particularly of the Catholic community, bring this killing to an end."

Neither side showed any sign of heeding Daly's call. Last week gunmen thought to be members of the I.R.A. narrowly missed killing a Protestant police reservist in an attack in County Armagh. Said the Rev. David Lapsley, a moderate Belfast Protestant: "I try to cultivate a dialogue, but long ago I gave up any notions that I was going to change attitudes dramatically." With 2,670 dead so far in

Civil rights demonstrators and the British Army in Londonderry, 1969

the conflict, few of Northern Ireland's 500,000 homes remain untouched by the loss of a child, a spouse, a friend or a workmate, someone murdered or wounded in a bomb blast or a spray of bullets. The numbers of the dead pale in comparison to the half million lives lost in the Iran-Iraq war or all those killed in Lebanon or Afghanistan. But proportionate to Ulster's 1.6 million population, 2,670 dead is the rough equivalent of 100,000 dead in Britain, twice that in Japan or 400,000 in the U.S. – more than enough to define a national tragedy.

Searching for the root of the conflict, some historians point back to the Anglo-Norman conquest of Ireland 800 years ago. Others trace the trouble to King James I, who from 1603 to 1625 granted large tracts of land in Ulster to Scottish and English colonizers. Protestant domination was established in 1690 at the Battle of the Boyne, when Dutch-born, Protestant King William of Orange prevailed over King James II, a Catholic who was struggling to regain his throne with Irish and French help.

But the bitter divisions of today belong, above all, to the people now living in the province. They remember the evening of Aug. 24, 1968, when 4,000 Catholics began a civil rights march in the mainly Roman Catholic village of Coalisland, County Tyrone. It seemed then no more than an Irish echo of the kind of movement that had swept across the U.S.

Chanting "We Shall Overcome", the marchers demanded equality in voting, housing and employment for Roman Catholics, who complained, with reason, of being the victims of an entrenched pattern of discrimination. The first skirmishes between Catholics and Protestants were fought with sticks and stones, a far cry from the deadly weaponry now available. In 1968 Northern Ireland had one of Europe's lowest crime rates; a murder trial was a rarity. Things soon changed. As a Protestant backlash grew,

British troops, arriving in August 1969, were welcomed, at least initially, by the Catholic population. The steady drone of British army helicopters became so familiar in Belfast that children learned to sleep through the sound. Heavily armed foot patrols hardly drew a glance from passersby in the street.

At the same time the I.R.A., demanding that Britain withdraw from Ulster, was gearing up for a long struggle. With that, the dynamics were in place for what would become perpetual violence.

Two decades later, the police station at Coalisland resembles a fortress, surrounded by thick walls and steel shutters. The civil rights protesters of the late '60s have grown middle-aged, and generally disapprove of the violence committed in the name of their cause. For many of the people, there is no answer to the conflict. Says Brian Feeney, a Belfast Catholic Councilor: "I don't see any likelihood of the I.R.A. stopping, but what people are asking is, What is the point of it all?" John Hume, once a Roman Catholic civil rights leader in Londonderry, now a member of both the British and European parliaments, says, "Our demands on votes and homes have been met. There still is a serious problem of jobs. Catholics are more than twice as likely to be out of work as Protestants. But I see absolutely no justification for violence." Yet the violence has spread like a spore.

What at first seemed a struggle concentrated in run-down Catholic enclaves of Belfast and Londonderry (Catholics call it Derry) has spilled into Britain, where more than 70 people died in I.R.A. bombings; to West Germany and the Netherlands, where British servicemen have become targets; to as far as Gibraltar, where members of Britain's Special Air Service regiment gunned down three I.R.A. members last March. Manhunts have prowled into the Irish Republic and back and forth across the 300-mile border. Sixty-foot British army watchtowers survey the northern side of the frontier; to the south, along the roads, Irish troops and police mount their own patrols.

Although the killing cycle grinds on, some people in Ulster detect a slowly changing atmosphere. There is a dogged spirit and a sense of pride that the outside world cannot see through the flames on television newsclips. The bars and restaurants of downtown Belfast are thronged on weekends. Businessmen have coined a marketing slogan to signal revival: "Belfast Is Buzzing." A $100 million shopping and office development is nearing completion on Royal Avenue, Belfast's main street; the city's general appearance has been spruced up. Departing from an expanded airport complex, holiday flights to Mediterranean resorts are filled to capacity. If hope in Northern Ireland is easily dismissed, it does exist – in the resilience of people on both sides, in a reviving commercial pace, in the swelling chorus of condemnation of yet another senseless killing.

5 *cessation* (U) (fml.): pause; end **19** *grievance* ['gri:vns]: cause for complaint • *trigger sth.:* start sth.; be the cause of a sudden reaction **26** *impassioned* (adj.): passionate, heartfelt **27** *plea* [pli:] (fml.): earnest request **35** *mourn sb./sth.* [mɔ:n ☆ mɔ:rn]: feel or express grief at the loss of sb./sth. **37** *Seamus* ['ʃeɪməs] **42** *retaliation* (U): Vergeltung **43** *ambush* (n.): surprise attack from a hidden place **51** *heed sb./sth.* (fml.): pay attention to sb./sth. **55** *Armagh* [ɑ:'mɑ:] **63** *spouse* [spaʊz ☆ spaʊs] (old-fashioned): husband or wife **85** *prevail over sb./sth.* (fml.): defeat sb./sth. **93–94** *Coalisland* [ˌkəʊl'aɪlənd] **94** *Tyrone* [tɪ'rəʊn] **102** *entrenched* (adj.): firmly established **103–104** *skirmish* ['skɜ:mɪʃ ☆ 'skɜ:r-] (n.): fight between small groups of people **110** *backlash:* extreme and violent reaction **121** *gear up for sb./sth.:* get ready for sb./sth. **157** *prowl* [praʊl]: move cautiously **163** *grind on:*

Belfast street scene, 1989

continue with slow power **165** *dogged* ['dɒgɪd ☆ 'dɔː-] (adj.): determined, stubborn **170** *throng sth.:* fill sth. with a crowd **176** *spruce sb./sth. up:* make sb./sth. tidy and clean **181** *resilience* [rɪ'zɪlɪəns] (U): Spannkraft, Zähigkeit

Talking about the text

1. Which long-term and short-term causes of the conflict in Northern Ireland are mentioned in the text?
2. How has everyday life been affected by the violence?
3. How does the situation today differ from that of the late sixties?
4. What are the chances, according to the authors, of the violence coming to an end in the near future?

INFO BOX

The Anatomy of the Conflict

Eight Centuries of Troubled History

Ever since the Normans invaded Ireland in the 12th century, England sought to fasten its hold of the island. In the early 17th century, when the Irish chieftains had been defeated, Scottish and English Protestant settlers were given land in the North of Ireland ("The plantation of Ulster"). English Protestant rule of Ireland was secured when King William of Orange defeated James – formerly King James II and a Catholic convert – at the Battle of the Boyne in 1690, an event still celebrated by Protestants in Northern Ireland with great ceremony today. In 1801, Ireland became part of the United Kingdom. Over the centuries there were several attempts on the part of the Irish to gain home rule – limited self-government –, but these failed until IRA (Irish Republican Army) guerrilla fighting led the British Government to agree to an Irish Free State in the South in 1921. Northern Ireland, i.e. the six counties with a Protestant majority, remained part of the UK and was given its own parliament at Stormont in Belfast. Electoral boundaries were drawn in a way that very much favoured Protestant candidates, and Roman Catholics were excluded from holding public office. Then in 1968, with the birth of the Civil Rights Movement, Ulster Catholics demanded the end to discrimination as regards housing, jobs and electoral rights.

<u>*The Troubles: A Sequence of Events*</u>

(For further information on political parties and other organizations mentioned in this list see below.)

1968 A Catholic civil rights march in Londonderry is attacked by the RUC (Royal Ulster Constabulary).

1969 A Catholic civil rights march is attacked by Protestants at Burntollet Bridge near Claudy. "Battle of the Bogside" in Londonderry. British troops are stationed in Belfast and Londonderry with the intention of preventing further violence.

1970 Division of the IRA and Sinn Féin into official and provisional (i.e. militant) sections as a result of increased violence by British troops. Riots in Belfast. The Provisional IRA (PIRA) begin their armed campaign. The B-Specials, reserve troops of the RUC, are disbanded and the UDR (Ulster Defence Regiment) is formed.

1971 The first British soldier is killed in the Troubles. Internment, i.e. imprisonment without trial, is introduced.

1972 13 civilians are shot dead by the army on "Bloody Sunday". The Northern Ireland parliament at Stormont/Belfast is suspended by the British Government and direct rule from Westminster imposed.

1973 PIRA bombing campaign in England. The Sunningdale conference agrees on a British, Irish and Northern Irish power-sharing executive.

1974 A Northern Ireland Executive is installed but is brought down by a Protestant general strike. Direct rule is reimposed.

1975 End of internment. Start of convicted Catholic terrorists' refusal to wear prison clothes and their demand to be treated as prisoners of war.

1976 The Women's Peace Movement (later known as the Peace People) is formed by two Roman Catholic women from Belfast, Máiread Corrigan and Betty Williams; in 1977 the movement is awarded the Nobel Peace Prize held over from 1976.

1980 300 prisoners join the "H-Block" protest (named after the shape of the cell block in which Catholic terrorists are held). Hunger strikes are begun and called off again in December.

1981 Bobby Sands, member of the PIRA and prisoner in the "H-Block", goes on hunger strike, is elected MP and dies, followed by nine fellow prisoners. PIRA bombing campaign in London.

1982 Northern Ireland Assembly: 78 seat parliament with consultative powers.

1983 Gerry Adams (Sinn Féin) elected as MP for West Belfast.

1984 PIRA bomb attack on Conservative Party leaders in Brighton, England.

1985 An Anglo-Irish agreement gives the Irish Government in Dublin a formal consultative role in the affairs of

Northern Ireland; the agreement is opposed by many Protestants.

1987 11 civilians are killed in a bomb explosion in Enniskillen; the PIRA claims responsibility and loses a lot of support as a result.

Political Parties in Northern Ireland

Ulster Unionist Party: This is the oldest and largest party in Northern Ireland. It is Protestant and pro-British and from 1921 to 1972 held the majority of seats in the Northern Ireland parliament.

Democratic Unionist Party (DUP): A break-away group from the Ulster Unionist Party, the DUP was founded in 1971 by the Reverend Ian Paisley and Desmond Boal. The decidedly Protestant party is opposed to any sharing of power with Catholics and to any links between Northern Ireland and the Republic of Ireland.

Alliance Party: Founded in 1970 to unite Roman Catholics and Protestants, this is a moderate, centre party.

Social Democratic and Labour Party (SDLP): The party, founded in 1970, speaks for the majority of Roman Catholics in Northern Ireland. It is left of centre and seeks the unification of Ireland through democratic and peaceful means.

Sinn Féin [ˌʃɪn ˈfeɪn]: The party was founded in 1905 to unite different competing nationalist groups in the struggle to win Irish independence. Today, Sinn Féin is the political wing of the Provisional IRA and seeks to justify the use of force to bring about a united Ireland. Although Sinn Féin is a legal party, its members are banned from discussing or being interviewed about their policies on T.V or radio.

Paramilitary Organizations

1. Anti-British Organizations

After the split in 1970 of the Irish Republican Army (IRA), there are now the *Official Irish Republican Army (OIRA)* (involved in violence until 1972), which wants to bring about change in a democratic way, and the *Provisional Irish Republican Army (PIRA).* The PIRA, which aims at a British withdrawal from Northern Ireland, is committed to guerrilla warfare and is the dominant element of violence in Northern Ireland.

The *Irish National Liberation Army (INLA)* is a violent group which broke away from the OIRA. It was involved in several bombings between 1979 and 1982.

OIRA, PIRA and INLA are banned by law.

2. Loyalist (pro-British) Organizations

The Protestant community has its own paramilitary organizations. Originally set up to defend the Protestants, they, too, have been involved in acts of violence.

The *Ulster Defence Association (UDA)* was set up in 1971. It supports the idea of an independent Ulster and is a legal organization. Those members of the UDA who indulge in acts of serious violence, including murder, do so under the name of *Ulster Freedom Fighters (UFF),* thus avoiding the UDA itself being banned.

The *Ulster Volunteer Force (UVF)* was founded in 1966. It took its name from a Protestant loyalist organization that existed from 1913 to 1920 and resisted self-government for Ireland. Today's UVF is committed to combating the Provisional IRA. It is an illegal organization.

3. Local Security Forces

The *Royal Ulster Constabulary (RUC)* is the Northern Ireland police force. Although precise figures do not exist, the RUC is estimated to be more than 80% Protestant.

The *Ulster Defence Regiment (UDR)* is a largely Protestant (97%) part-time armed loyalist defence force. It was formed in 1970 under the control of the British Army.

2

Alf McCreary
Between the Lines

Singling out the main factors in the Northern Irish conflict, the journalist Alf McCreary, from whose book *Tried by Fire* (1986) the following excerpt is taken, offers an analysis of the present situation.

Part of the tragedy is that the conflict feeds on itself. Today's generation of young people has grown up in a political wilderness that is pockmarked by bomb and bullet. Many children are the prisoners of their own environment and are programmed by their background to support one side or the other. There are, of course, children and parents who take the positive view and who try to escape from the shackles of the past to bring some objectivity to the present. But the peace-makers in Ireland, North and South, face a formidable task in trying to nurture the tender plant of reason and understanding in a cold and often hostile climate.

Another contributory factor in the Irish conflict is that each person, like each group, sees that conflict in his or her own terms. The Northern Protestant argues that he has the democratic majority in Northern Ireland and that he therefore has the right to majority rule. And he would regard the aspirations of Northern Roman Catholics for a United Ireland as nothing less than treachery and a lack of loyalty to the Northern state.

The Southern Republican would argue that the Northern Protestant is less than reasonable in refusing to share the top positions of power and influence with Northern Catholics in a Belfast-based government which would have certain powers transferred from Westminster. Furthermore he would point out that this system of devolved or transferred government had not worked properly and that the real root of the Irish conflict is the Northern Protestant's stubbornness in refusing to take part in an all-Ireland government. Why should one million Northerners, who are a minority on the island, hold out against the wishes of a majority of people in Ireland?

In reply the Northerner would say that he does not trust the Southerner and that he is afraid of entering into partnership in a State which is so heavily disposed to the power of the Roman Catholic Church. Whether these fears are justified or not is scarcely the point, disappointing though that might seem. In Ireland, North and South, and for all kinds of Irishmen and women it is important to know the relevance ot Murphy's Law of Communication: "What people believe to be the truth is more potent and often more dangerous than the truth itself."

So the old arguments continue, often with only a nodding acquaintance with the true facts of history and contemporary events. But the impact of this partial view of Irish affairs cannot be over-estimated.

(This was demonstrated forcibly on a study-tour to Holland by six journalists from Northern Ireland and six from the Republic. Three each were asked to take over the roles of management, Press, trade unions and international directors in an imaginary take-over of a local firm by a multi-national. After an evening of intensive role-playing, the authenticity of which surprised even those hard-bitten professionals, the message was made clear by the Dutch hosts – each group in the game was seeing the conflict only in its own terms. No-one had been able to stand back and take the global view. The parallel with the Irish conflict was all too real.)

In Ireland the conflict is so complex that people will disagree about the relative importance of the contributory factors. Some will point to religion, others to cultural differences, others to economics, and others still to political conflicts. Some will list more than one cause, but in different degrees of importance. Any simple analysis is distrusted mainly because it seems too simple. The Irish are a rhetorical race who look for complexities that will measure up to their eloquence. As the British and others have found out, if something appears simple the Irish will soon make it complicated.

Orangemen marching through Belfast on their annual 12th July parade

Religion is a factor in the conflict, though some churchmen would claim that this is over-stressed. Certainly there is a broad agreement that the fight is not about theology as such. The days are gone when people are burned at the stake for a refusal to accept a tenet of what is thought to be the true faith. It is beyond dispute that stone-throwing mobs in Belfast and Londonderry are not pelting one another or the police to make a point about the Virgin Birth or transubstantiation.

It would be misleading to suggest, however, that religion is not therefore a factor to be taken seriously. There are many Protestants who would be fearful, rightly or wrongly, of the influence of the Roman Catholic Church and who see the Irish conflict in terms of a Vatican conquest that has to be resisted at all costs. There is, equally, a Roman Catholic mistrust and fear of a Protestant majority in a Northern state that would favour

Presbyterians, Anglicans and Methodists at the expense of Roman Catholics. And in an all-Ireland context, Northern Protestants could look with distrust on a theocracy where divorce is prohibited and contraception is limited.

Thus if religion in the conflict is not strictly theological, it is certainly tribal. In Northern Ireland the terms "Roman Catholic" and "Protestant" immediately suggest different backgrounds, cultures and values. The Catholic is likely to have been given a thorough grounding in history as seen from a Catholic Irish point of view, and to speak, to whatever degree, the Irish language. He or she is likely to play or have played essentially Irish games like Gaelic football, hurling, and camogie.

The Protestant, by contrast, is likely to have a grounding in history as seen from a British point of view and is unlikely to be able to speak even a smattering of the Irish language, or to play Gaelic games. Of course there are exceptions. Some Protestants speak Gaelic, some Catholics will have gone to a Protestant school and will have read history through Protestant eyes. Protestants and Catholics share a number of sports and activities, particularly in middle-class areas and professions. But in the main the cultural divide between Protestants and Catholics remains.

It is immensely sad that such a degree of mutual ignorance still exists. One of the major problems of Northern Ireland and of Ireland as a whole is that so few people know how the others live. This is particularly clear to me as I cross the barriers in the North, and often the Irish border into the South. It is fair to say that many in the Republic who talk about Irish unity have not been to the North and know little or nothing about the Northern Protestant. In the same vein, the Unionists in the North who cling to loyalty to Britain are not knowledgeable about the South, though more seem to travel to the Republic than Southerners to the North.

In the North itself the mutual ignorance of both communities about one another is depressing. This may not be apparent to those who pontificate from the familiarity of their own backgrounds and who remain fortified by their own herd instinct. But to me, this mutual lack of knowledge is very apparent. A reporter can sit in the Catholic Bogside of Derry and take tea with an unemployed Derry man who will talk with passion and conviction about the rights and wrongs of history and the brighter future in a united Ireland. The same reporter the next day can sit in Protestant East Belfast and take tea with an unemployed ship-builder who will talk with equal conviction and passion about the rights and wrongs of history and about the advantages of maintaining the link with Britain.

One particular meeting with a Catholic Derryman and a Protestant from Belfast was, for me, a salutary lesson. During dinner they talked about work and the lack of work in Northern Ireland. They found out, as working men, they had much in common but once they switched to politics the barriers went up and there was no more communication. They were talking at one another and not to one another, and sadly they symbolised the division between their communities which, on a purely economic basis in a deprived part of the United Kingdom, have so much in common, namely unemployment and lower living standards than in the rest of the United Kingdom.

Some observers have put forward the view that this economic deprivation has contributed to the conflict. They would claim that cultural and community differences are highlighted in an area where jobs are scarce and that part of the conflict at least is due to the destructive power of those who have little to lose anyway. Put crudely the argument is that a man with a good job, a nice home and a car is less likely to take up a gun than a man who is permanently unemployed and who sees himself as being outside

the established system of earning-power and social acceptance and who has little chance of ever getting a job.

It is true that there is a definite class-pattern in the kind of people who have been convicted for crimes of violence. The majority tend to be from the working-class and there are relatively few from the professions. A bomber is more likely to be, for example, an unemployed labourer than a solicitor. On the other hand the class argument does not explain away the loyalty to Britain that is expressed right across the spectrum of Protestant classes. Where else but in Northern Ireland could be seen a working-class accordion band dedicated to a peer of the realm? He lived in the country grandeur of an estate nearly a hundred miles from the little terraced homes of shipbuilders who had nothing more in common with the object of their dedication than loyalty to Protestantism, as understood by Ulster Protestants.

Whatever the relative importance of religion, culture and economics in the Northern Ireland conflict, it is certain that the political dimension is the tip of the ice-berg. This is the problem in its most uncompromising form. The one million Northern Protestants have expressed their desire to remain British. The half-million Northern Catholics have looked towards an all-Ireland context. So far the British and the Ulster Protestant have failed to work out a system in the North to satisfy everyone. Recent events have indicated that the British government may be looking more to the Irish Government to try to bring some stability to the North, but this in itself creates the danger of a Northern Protestant backlash in retaliation against any attempts at a solution which would endanger their position in the North.

Behind all these factors, including the political dimension, lies the greatest unsolved crisis in the North – the lack of a collective identity. The Protestant feels he is British but also Irish. The Catholic feels he is Irish, though not quite the same as the Southern Irish. But as yet there is no shared Northern identity, which is to be British and Irish in a different kind of way to the majority in Britain and Ireland but not to feel totally British or totally Irish. This possibility of fostering, long-term, a new Northern identity that is acceptable to Roman Catholics and Protestants may contain the seeds of future peace and stability.

5 *shackles* (pl.) (fig.): conditions that prevent one from acting or speaking freely **7** *formidable:* difficult to deal with or overcome • *nurture sb./sth.* ['nɜːtʃə ☆ 'nɜːrtʃər]: care for sb., encourage the growth of sth. **8** *hostile* ['hɒstaɪl ☆ 'hɑːstl]: very unfriendly **12** *aspiration:* strong desire or ambition **13** *treachery* ['tretʃərɪ ☆ -riː]: act of betraying a person or cause **18** *devolve sth.* (fml.): transfer sth. (e.g. power or authority) from central government to regional authorities **24** *be desposed to sb./sth.:* be inclined to think that sb./sth. is good or worthwhile **30** *nodding* (adj.): (here) slight **31** *partial* ['pɑːʃl ☆ 'pɑːrʃl]: incomplete **37** *hard-bitten:* tough, strong **46** *measure up to sb./sth.:* meet the requirements of sb./sth. • *eloquence* (U): skilful use of expressive language **50** *stake:* in former times, post to which person was tied to be burnt alive **51** *tenet* ['– –]: principle; belief; doctrine **52** *pelt sb./sth.:* strike at sb./sth. with missiles **59** *Presbyterians, Anglicans and Methodists:* members of different Protestant churches (cf. "Info-Box", p. 10) • *at the expense of sb./sth.:* with loss or damage to sb./sth. **60** *theocracy* [θɪ'ɒkrəsɪ ☆ θɪ'ɑːkrəsiː]:

(country with a) system of government by priests in which the laws of the state are believed to be the laws of God **61** *divorce* [dɪ'vɔːs ☆ -'vɔːrs]: Ehescheidung • *contraception* (U): Empfängnisverhütung **62** *tribal* ['traɪbl] (adj.): of or belonging to a certain community or racial group **65** *grounding* (n.): teaching of the basic elements of a subject **66** *Irish language:* Celtic language of Ireland (cf. "Info-Box", p. 44) **67** *hurling* ['hɜːlɪŋ ☆ 'hɜːr-], *and camogie* [kə'məʊgɪ] (U): Irish ball games similar to hockey **69** *smattering* (n.): slight knowledge, especially of a language **75** *mutual* ['mjuːtʃʊəl]: gegenseitig **80** *vein* [veɪn]: manner, style • *cling to sb./sth.:* be very attached to sb./sth. **84** *pontificate:* speak as if one were the only person who knew the facts about sth. **85** *fortify sb./sth.:* streng then sb./sth. **86** *Bogside:* Catholic area of Londonderry **88** *conviction:* firm belief **94** *salutary* ['sæljʊtrɪ ☆ -jəteriː]: having a good effect **98** *deprived* (adj.): without adequate food, housing, health care etc. **103** *scarce* [skeəs ☆ skeərs]: rare **104** *crude:* rough, unskilful **119** *dedicate sth. to sb.:* address sth. to sb. as a way of showing respect • *peer:* (in Britain) male member of the nobility **120** *realm* [relm] (fml.): kingdom **131** *retaliation* (U): Vergeltung **138** *foster sth.* ['fɒstə ☆ 'fɔːstər]: help the growth or development of sth.

Talking about the text

1. The author talks about two fundamentally different views of the conflict. What are these views and who holds them?
2. Explain in your own words what is meant by "Murphy's Law of Communication" (ll. 27–28) and show how, according to McCreary, it applies to the Irish situation.
3. What importance, in the author's view, do religious differences have in the conflict?
4. What part does the economic situation in Northern Ireland play in the unrest?
5. McCreary mentions the need to foster "a new Northern identity" (l. 138). Explain what he means by this and suggest how this aim might be achieved.

3
The Troubles in the Press

The media in Great Britain are often as divided about the Northern Irish conflict as the general public. The *Daily Mirror* and *Today*, two popular London-based newspapers, offer very different views of Northern Ireland's situation 20 years after the stationing of British troops.

a) *Daily Mirror* (August 10, 1989):
Twenty years ago, British troops were sent to Northern Ireland to keep the peace. There is still no peace and there can be no peace while they are there.

On August 14, 1969, Harold Wilson's Labour government dispatched the troops to stop the Protestants terrorising the Catholics. Successive governments have believed, sincerely but mistakenly, that "there will be a bloodbath" if the troops leave.

Yet every 12 days, on average, a British soldier or Ulster Defence Regiment volunteer has been killed. So have nearly 2,000 civilians and 263 members of the Royal Ulster Constabulary. That IS a bloodbath. [...]

Bigotry: Britain cannot solve the Irish problem because we caused it with partition in 1921 and we are still part of it.

A settlement cannot be reached until Britain has withdrawn, totally, from Ireland. That would compel all the people – North and South – to work together to build a new and peaceful nation.

That would strip the IRA of the bulk of its support. Its existence depends on being able to inflame emotions against the old British enemy. In a united Ireland few would follow its failed Marxist atheism.

That is the only way out of continuing bigotry, hatred, anarchy and murder.

Much has changed in 20 years. Britain and the Republic are bound together as partners in the European Community, which guarantees fair treatment, human rights and justice. The new problems of Ireland would be open to a European solution.

It wouldn't be weakness for Britain to leave. It would be strength. It is the only path to permanent peace.

Must thousands more be murdered in Ulster before a British Government has the vision to see it?

Robert Maxwell, Publisher

---

b) *Today* (August 11, 1989):
There are those who sneer at Ulster and would wash their hands of it and its people.

To them, Northern Ireland is an expensive problem they don't even start to understand. All they want is to be rid of it.

Top of the list of these sneerers and handwringers is the *Daily Mirror*, which is as treacherous to the people of Ulster as it is ill-informed.

Yesterday in a front-page editorial it called, as it has done many times before, for the withdrawal not just of troops but of a British presence.

The people who run the *Daily Mirror* and write such undiluted garbage do so from their mink-lined ivory tower in London.

All they know of the situation in Northern Ireland they have learned from the tatty pages of their own illiterate rag.

Along with their glasses of chilled white wine they swallow whole the propaganda of thugs, gunmen, bombers and political loudmouths.

They don't know the reality of life in Ulster because they wouldn't dream of visiting it. They don't recognise the achievements of the province because they want to believe the blackest picture possible.

The *Mirror* can only chronicle the 20 years since British troops moved in as a catalogue of blood and tears. Yet there has been so much more.

Over the same period Ulster has undergone a remarkable transformation. It has become a land of rejuvenation, boom and increasing prosperity. A place where a growing number of citizens live in harmony.

All of that has only been possible because of the ordinary people of Ulster who have through their own enterprise, initiative and drive dragged their homeland back from the brink and set it on the road to a new prosperity. [...]

Before the Czech-born Maxwell bought the *Mirror* his only claim to political fame was as a short-term Labour MP.

It is too easy to laugh at him, though. What he demands for Ulster is not a joke. It would condemn the province and its people to life under the murderous rule of gangs of psychopaths who falsely claim to represent one side or the other.

The six counties would become no better than Sicily, with a population living in terror of the Mafia.

These are the bedfellows with whom the *Mirror* is sleeping. Through ignorance and stupidity it supports gangsters and gunmen, and a policy that could lead to genocide.

Today's support is not for the tiny minority of killers and hate-filled monsters. We back the decent majority who have the same feelings, hopes and ideals as all other UK citizens.

The *Daily Mirror* cannot see that it too should be on that side. Thus it condemns itself as a traitor to the cause of peace in Ulster and to the richer future the people deserve.

The *Mirror* should be shunned and boycotted. It is no worthy companion on the road to a better tomorrow.

6 *Harold Wilson* (1916–): British Labour prime minister (1964–1970, 1974 bis 1976) **7** *dispatch sb./sth.:* send sb./sth. off to a destination or for a special purpose **19** *bigotry* ['– – –] (U): intolerant or narrowminded attitude or behaviour **21** *partition in 1921:* cf. "Info-Box", p. 17 **22** *settlement:* agreement **27** *bulk of sth.:* most of sth. **49** *sneer at sb./sth.:* show contempt for sb./sth. **50** *wash one's hands of sb./sth.* (fig.): refuse to be responsible for sb./sth. (any longer) **65** *undiluted* [ˌʌndaɪ'ljuːtɪd ☆ -'luː-] (adj.): pure **66** *mink-lined* (adj.): nerzgefüttert; (hier) bequem, luxuriös **70** *tatty* (infml.): shabby; cheap **70–71** *illiterate* [ɪ'lɪtərət]: showing little or no education; ignorant **71** *rag* (infml., derog.): newspaper or journal **74** *thug:* violent criminal; hooligan **114** *genocide* ['dʒenəsaɪd]: Völkermord **125** *shun sb./sth.:* avoid sb./sth.; keep away from sb./sth.

Talking about the texts

1. What arguments does the publisher of the *Daily Mirror* present for Britain leaving Northern Ireland and what, according to him, would be the result of this withdrawal?
2. How does the commentator of *Today* respond to these arguments?
3. Comment on the general approach and the style of the two articles.
4. Which of the two articles do you find more convincing? Give reasons for your answer.

4

Linda Anderson
If in Doubt, Shoot

In this excerpt from Linda Anderson's novel *To Stay Alive* (1984) a young British soldier looks at Belfast and the Troubles, trying to make sense of his conflicting experiences.

Belfast was suffocating. It made him long for open country; somewhere to breathe free and deep. The city was flanked on three sides by mountains, a huge cemetery overhanging its north side. Like an omen. Or a comment. He must not keep looking up at the hills. Whence cometh no help. Must keep alert. Trust no one, as he had been warned. He stood at the observation post and watched the milling bodies. The people looked sullen. Or scared. Or just dog-tired. It was late 1979. They had been fighting for eleven years! Sometimes Gerry felt he was in a slum area like any other; sometimes it was like another planet. When he first arrived there, he had gone mad with his camera till he was stopped. ("They'll think it's intelligence-gathering, you fool. If you want to take snapshots, come back as a tourist.") But he had quite a collection of photographs, an evangelist wearing a plastic bib covered with a Bible text, "When the wicked perisheth, there is shouting"; some Orangemen holding aloft a Temperance banner; a wall covered with chilling messages: FTQ, which turned out to be a shorthand exhortation to commit an extraordinary act with Her Majesty; "What's blue and flies through the air? Louis Mountbatten." It was that kind of raw gloating hatred that frightened him most in this country.

In his first week there was a spate of tit-for-tat killings. Every dawn brought to light some pathetic corpse dumped somewhere. Police and ambulance men would descend quickly to remove it. They looked stonyfaced, accustomed, as if they were sweeping up McDonald's litter. Two of the Catholic victims were killed without resort to guns or knives. Beaten and kicked to death, their faces squashed into mincemeat. Gerry couldn't stop thinking about that. It seemed that mere killing wasn't enough punishment, couldn't assuage that hatred. The assassins had to make the most of it, a prolonged operation. As if with every kick and blow they were saying, "I mean it! I mean it!" But how could you hate a stranger so much that you wanted to stamp out his very face? Gerry thought that if he had to kill someone it would have to be as quick and neat as possible. Scientific. Any long slow process always aroused doubts and regrets in him, even the wooing of a girl or the reading of a book. So how could those men not wonder in the middle of doing someone in? Why were they not moved by the man's cries? What made them so certain? It was awesome. He wondered how people could endure that level of fear? They seemed resigned to it. "Murder is respectable in Ireland," said Des. "It's sex that's the real shocker!" He made a face of mock horror. "You know that cinema we passed yesterday? The de luxe fleapit? They're showing a porno film, right?"

"Do you want to go to it?"

"There's a better show outside! Remember all those people we thought were queuing to get in? They're bloody picketing it twenty-four hours a day! They stand there singing hymns. It would be a brave punter that would try and get past them, I tell you. There's even a contingent from the Upward Bound Club."

"You're making it up," Gerry said in the middle of a fit of giggles. He was always giggling. Des had to thump him to make him stop.

Gerry had not been prepared at all for Ulster, although officially he was fully prepared. He thought now that being born there might be the only real preparation! He remembered the briefing lectures he attended during his "internal security" special training, so-called, at Lydd. They were given a potted history of Ireland: eight hundred years of horror and counter-horror explained in three hours. "Potty" history the officer joked, while the squaddies guffawed obediently. It was like school where you listened not to what the teacher said but to how he said it, so that you could laugh on cue, look impressed on cue.

British soldier in front of an IRA mural

Anyway, none of the beautifully mapped history made sense now that he was here. He was supposed to be in Belfast to keep the peace. Isolate the gunmen. That was a nice phrase. Made the gunmen sound like some manageable quantity. But they were legion, swarms, unbreakable. And didn't wear any identifying insignia! Every man was a gunman, or a supporter of gunmen. The support was rarely only verbal. Even preschool kids threw stones at soldiers, collected milk bottles for the production of petrol bombs.

So it didn't make sense that he was there to protect the Catholics from the Protestants which was one of the garbled justifications he had heard. You were safe in Protestant areas. The Catholics were your enemies. There were so many ghastly warnings about them: the story of the hospitable lady who gave sandwiches to some soldiers. The filling was powdered glass. The kids who collected autographs of IRA gunmen ... They wanted to kill you. They did not want your protection. The Protestants were British like you. More than you. Their houses were bedecked with Union Jacks. There were pictures of the Queen in their parlours. Also Philip, Anne, Charles, Mark Phillips. But not Margaret. She was too flighty.

Gerry and Des went to the Martyrs' Memorial, attracted by the orational fame of Ian Paisley. The service began with a few hymns full of stuff about the battle, striving, not resting. A few Jesus jingles. Then Paisley rose.

They watched the black bulk of the man as he paced back and forth, brandishing a Bible above his head. "This is not a book of peace! This is a book of war! Jesus was no softie! 'I come to bring you not peace but a sword.'"

A lot of words about hell's busy bonfires that depended on supplies of infidels, sinners and Papists. Hell seemed to be a place built to the satisfaction of Protestants. When the audience was all worked up into a lather, he boomed at them: "Come, come to the Lord." Gerry watched the lewd devout faces of women who were coming, coming to the Lord all right.

Outside after the service the congregation looked like sane and worthy citizens. The Protestants. Our allies. Yet, these were the people who brought the country to a standstill with a general strike in 1974 to bring down a power-sharing experiment. To defy the British government ... But you were safe in their areas. The Catholics were your joint enemy. At Lydd there was a model ramshackle town nicknamed "Tin City" where the soldiers had to conduct mock battles and arrests as part of their training. Gerry had enjoyed it. It made the conflict less real, not more, like a Hollywood film set. One of the exercises involved one group of men pretending to be Protestants taking part in a funeral procession while a group of "Catholics" tried to steal the coffin.

Did Catholics do such things? Why?

There was a lecture on the IRA. Their weapons, tactics, ideology, structure. There were the theorists, Sinn Fein, and the military, Provisional IRA, "the mouth and muscle ends of the the business", the officer said. The IRA had once had a structure which was a replica of the British army with regiments, battalions, titles, ranks, training, and strict discipline. They had now changed to a cellular structure. There were separate independent units each responsible in an area for a single activity: bombings, executions, bank robberies... The aim was to diminish the amount of information that could be "extracted" from any caught IRA man.

It sounded clever. The IRA were disciplined, dedicated, and clever.

Not as they were portrayed in *Soldier* mag. every week where the cartoon man Seamus could be relied upon to blow himself up or shoot himself by accident. That was as true as an army recruiting ad!

They were shown a film about IRA atrocities. The final shot was of a woman speaking at a graveside: "We'll bury our sons and daughters and we shall be *proud*."

Then followed the usual homily by the officer. "Despite all of this viciousness, the general population continues to support them."

Des raised his hand.

The officer blinked in confusion. "What is it, man?"

"Why?"

"Why what? Oh... because a lot of Irish are mindless fanatics. Easily led by politicians and priests. George Bernard Shaw, and he was Irish himself so he knew what he was talking about, he said: 'Put an Irishman on the spit, and you will always find another Irishman to turn him.'" He beamed down with brotherly love on his own compatriots by way of contrast.

"Mindless fanatics," Gerry thought. "Mindless. That's what you think about us, too. *Sans* 'O' levels, *sans* everything."

He felt queasy when he received his yellow card. Licence to kill. It listed the circumstances in which he was allowed to aim fire.

If he identified a sniper or a petrol-bomber.

If his life or another life was in danger.

After giving a warning.

He was to use only one round.

It would take ten minutes to go through that rigmarole. "Will the other fella wait while I shout, 'Halt, who goes there', and all of that? I'd have more holes in me than a bloody colander."

"Your yellow card is more for your PR," the sergeant told him. "Listen, if they've got petrol bombs, shoot them. If you're sure they've got a gun, shoot them. If in doubt, shoot."

1 *suffocating* (adj.): causing difficulty in breathing **4** *Whence cometh no help* (biblical lang.): where no help comes from • *alert* [ə'lɜːt ☆ -'lɜːrt] (adj.): watchful **5** *mill* (v.): (of people or animals) move round and round in a mass **6** *sullen* (adj.): gloomy, ill-humoured **9** *intelligence-gathering* (n.): collecting of information of military value **11** *bib:* Latz, Lätzchen • *perisheth* (biblical lang.) = *perishes:* dies **12** *Orangeman:* member of the Orange Society, an organization founded in 1795 to preserve Protestantism in Northern Ireland; so-called after King William of Orange (cf. "Info-Box", p. 21) • *aloft* [– '–]: up in the air; overhead • *Temperance banner:* large rectangular flag bearing the motto of the Orange Society (cf. l. 12), "No Surrender" **13** *chilling* (adj.): frightening • *FTQ* (abbr.) = *Fuck the Queen* (vulg.) • *exhortation:* earnest request **14–15** *Louis Mountbatten* (1900–1979): British admiral, killed when his boat was blown up by the IRA off the west coast of Ireland **15** *gloat:* express or feel selfish delight at sb. else's misfortune **17** *spate* (v.): outburst • *tit-for-tat* (adj.): revengeful **20–21** *resort to sth.*[rɪ'zɔːt ☆ -'zɔːrt] (n.): use of sth. **23** *assuage sth.* [ə'sweɪdʒ] (fml.): lessen the intensity of sth. **28** *woo sb.* (old-fashioned): try to persuade sb. to marry one **29** *do sb. in* (sl.): kill sb. **33** *fleapit* (BE infml.): old and shabby cinema or theatre **37** *picket sth.:* block the entrance of sth. as a form of protest (e.g. in a strike) **38** *punter* ['pʌntə ☆ -tər] (BE infml.): foolish person who takes risks **39** *Upward Bound Club* (derog): (here) Christian movement **44** *briefing* (n.): final instructions or necessary information **45** *Lydd:* small town in Northern Ireland • *potted* (adj.) (derog.): short and simplified **46** *potty* (BE infml.): foolish, crazy **47** *squaddie* (BE infml.): soldier • *guffaw* [gə'fɔː] (derog.): laugh loudly or in a vulgar manner **48** *on cue* [kjuː]: at exactly the expected moment **75** *garbled* (adj.): confused and misleading **89** *bedeck sb./sth.:* decorate sb./sth. **91** *flighty:* irresponsible, silly

92 *Martyrs' Memorial:* Free Presbyterian Church of which Ian Paisley (cf. ll. 90–91) is the minister **92–93** *Ian Paisley* (1926–): Northern Irish Protestant clergyman, strong adversary of Catholicism, member of the House of Commons for the Ulster Democratic Unionist Party (1970–) and member of the European Parliament (1979–) **93** *strive – strove – striven:* try hard, struggle **94** *jingle:* short catchy tune or song **95** *brandish sth.:* wave sth. about threateningly **98** *bonfire* large fire in the open •*infidel* ['ɪnfɪdəl]:disbeliever **99** *Papist* (derog.): Roman Catholic **100** *lather* (infml.): agitated, angry state **101** *lewd* [ljuːd ☆ luːd]: lustful • *devout* [dɪ'vaʊt]: religious, pious **106** *power-sharing experiment:* reference to the Sunningdale Agreement of 1974 (cf. "Info-Box", p. 22) **107** *defy sb./sth.:* resist sb./sth. boldly or openly **110** *ramshackle:* old and in need of repair **123** *Sinn Fein* [ˌʃɪn 'feɪn]: political wing of the Provisional IRA (cf. "Info-Box", p. 23) **124** *Provisional IRA* (abbr.) = *Provisional Irish Republican Army:* militant organization of Irish nationalists (cf. "Info-Box", p. 23) **125** *replica* ['replɪkə]: exact copy **131** *"Soldier" mag.* (abbr.) = *"Soldier" magazine:* magazine for members of the British Army • *Seamus* ['ʃeɪməs]: popular male name (usu. of Catholics) in Ireland **134** *atrocity* [– '– – –]: wicked or cruel act **136** *homily* ['hɒmɪlɪ ☆ 'hɑːmɪliː]: sermon, moralizing speech • *viciousness* (U): badness, evil **142** *George Bernard Shaw* (1856–1950): Irish playwright, critic and writer on social and political subjects **143** *spit:* Spieß **144** *beam down on sb.:* smile at sb. **147** *sans* [sã] (Fr.): without **148** *queasy:* slightly sick **150** *sniper:* gunman who shoots from cover and at long range **153** *round:* single shot from a rifle **154** *rigmarole* ['rɪgmərəʊl] (derog.): long and confusing list **156** *colander* ['kʌləndə ☆ -dər]: Seiher, Sieb **157** *PR* (abbr.) = *public relations* (pl.): work of presenting a good image of an organization

Talking about the text

1. How does the protagonist feel about Belfast and its people?
2. Sum up Gerry's views on the Northern Irish conflict.
3. "Gerry had not been prepared for Ulster, although officially he was fully prepared" (l. 42). Explain this statement and give examples from the text.
4. What stylistic means does the author use to show Gerry's thoughts and emotions?

5

Padraic Fiacc
Enemy Encounter

The following poem describes a chance meeting between a Northern Irish civilian and a British soldier.

for Lilac

Dumping (left over from the autumn)
Dead leaves, near a culvert
I come on
                    a British Army Soldier
With a rifle and a radio
Perched hiding. He has red hair.

He is young enough to be my weenie
-bopper daughter's boy-friend.
He is like a lonely little winter robin.

We are that close to each other, I
Can nearly hear his heart beating.

I say something bland to make him grin,
But his glass eyes look past my side
-whiskers down
                    the Shore Road street.
I am an Irish man
                    and he is afraid
That I have come to kill him.

encounter: sudden or unexpected meeting **3** *culvert* ['kʌlvət ☆ -vərt]: Abflußgraben **6** *radio:* apparatus for sending and receiving messages by electromagnetic waves **7** *perch:* sit, especially on sth. high or narrow; (of a bird) come to rest or stay (e.g. on a branch) **8–9** *weenie-bopper* (adj.) (infml.): of or belonging to a young teenager **10** *robin:* Rotkehlchen **13** *bland:* casual in manner; pleasant, but superficial **16** *Shore Road:* road in Belfast

CHAPTER III

Daily Life in Northern Ireland

1

FRANK DAVIES

Life Goes On in "Neutral Zone"

In a newspaper article American journalist Frank Davies compares life in Belfast with that in other big towns and cities in Europe. The result, he finds, is promising.

Angela Burns and three of her friends spent an evening the way thousands of Europeans did. They took advantage of late shopping hours at a department store to make purchases, ate at an Indian restaurant, then joined the crowd at a boisterous pub.

Nothing unusual, except that Burns' downtown is a "control zone" in which parked cars are banned to prevent bombings, where burned-out warehouses still dot the landscape and armored personnel carriers with British soldiers guard a courthouse ringed in barbed wire.

But Burns was surprised at the suggestion that there was any danger in working, shopping and drinking in her hometown of Belfast.

"You know, we're not all bomb throwers here," said Burns, a sales clerk, as she sipped a cocktail in the Drury Lane bar, named for a street in London's theater district. "This isn't like London, but the city center is getting better. We have our troubles, but life goes on."

Belfast isn't London, but it's not Beirut either, and Burns' feisty pride in her community symbolizes the resilience and economic progress of a downtown better known for car bombs and urban blight.

Belfast is the capital of Ulster, a British province wracked by 17 years of vicious fighting between Roman Catholic and Protestant extremists, their supporters and the police and British Army.

While extremists make news with violence and tribal parades, downtown Belfast is experiencing a quiet resurgence generated by large development grants from the Government, its unofficial status as a neutral zone by the thousands of Roman Catholics and Protestants who work and shop there – and an unexpected by-product of urban terrorism.

Banning cars from the city center all but ended the random bombings of the 1970s and at the same time created instant pedestrian malls. When street violence subsided about three years ago, retail business picked up and several large department stores began to stay open later one night a week. The experiment was an immediate success.

Major retailers such as London-based Marks and Spencer's, which spent US $30 million, refurbished their buildings. New specialty clothing and electronics stores opened along Franklin Street. Development funds – provided by Prime Minister Margaret Thatcher's government to demonstrate that Britain is not about to abandon the Province – and European Economic Community grants have helped to pay for many of the improvements.

This summer the Grand Opera, a magnificent Victorian building recently renovated for US $4.5 million, offers popular performances most nights. After the show, the crowds head for new fashionable pubs such as the Drury Lane and the Beaten Docket along the "Golden Mile" of Great Victoria Street.

"Through the Troubles (as the sectarian violence is known) many of these buildings were bombed out, but now they've been fixed up and business is good," said Paddy McAnerney, manager of the Drury Lane.

Perhaps the best measure of some normality returning to the area is Wimpy's, Britain's equivalent of McDonald's or Burger King, which just opened around the corner from the City Hall. The fast-food restaurant signified that downtown was safe for families, the core of its business.

It's a five minute walk from Wimpy's, with happy, ketchup-smeared children munching on french fries, to the great, gray City Hall. A huge banner draped across the entrance – "Belfast Says No" – is a reminder that militant Protestants control the City Council, and they have totally rejected the Anglo-Irish accord.

It also is a reminder of just how fragile this revitalized downtown can be. Resentment and despair always are ready to

Shopping in Belfast's Donegall Place

burst into violence in the Catholic and Protestant slums just a few kilometers away, where more than 50 per cent of the adults have no jobs.

This summer's round of marches and demonstrations, with Protestant extremists showing that they can match the Irish Republican Army for brutality and retribution, might spark a new cycle of violence that could cripple Belfast.

James Arnold, 29, an unemployed textile engineer who works odd jobs and occasionally drives a taxi, expressed the hopes and fears for his hometown's future.

"I've been heartened by what's happening downtown," said Arnold, a Protestant, "but these Troubles are just so stupid, can you believe that this would go on so long? Sometimes I think we're bent on self-destruction."

7 *boisterous:* noisily cheerful **9** *downtown* (AE) = (BE) *city centre* **12** *dot sth.:* be scattered over sth. • *armored* (AE) = (BE) *armoured* [ˈ– –] (adj.): protected by metal plates **12–13** *personnel carrier* [ˌpɜːsəˈnel ☆ ˌpɜːr-]: military vehicle carrying soldiers **14** *barbed wire:* Stacheldraht **27** *feisty* [ˈfiːstɪ ☆ ˈfaɪstiː] (AE infml.): passionate; energetic **28** *resilience* [rɪˈzɪlɪəns] (U): ability to recover quickly from misfortune or disturbance **30** *blight* (U) (fig.): disorder or decay **32** *wrack sth.:* destroy sth. **37** *tribal* [ˈtraɪbl] (adj.): of or belonging to a certain community or racial group **38** *resurgence* [rɪˈsɜːdʒəns ☆ -ˈsɜːr-] (U): revival; new activity **45** *all but:* almost **46** *random:* without a definite pattern or without regularity **48** *pedestrian mall* [pɪˌdestrɪən ˈmɔːl] (AE): shopping area banned for cars **49** *subside* [– ˈ–]: become less intense **49–50** *retail business* [ˈ– – ˌ– –] (U): Einzelhandel **50** *pick up:* recover activity **56** *refurbish sth.* [ˌrɪˈfɜːbɪʃ ☆ -ˈfɜːr-]: renovate sth. **84** *City Hall:* building containing local government offices **86** *core:* centre; most important part of sth. **90** *munch on sth.:* chew noisily on sth. • *french fries* (AE) = (BE) *chips* **91** *banner:* large rectangular flag or strip of cloth **91–92** *drape sth. across sth.:* hang sth. (e.g. cloth) loosely across sth. **95** *Anglo-Irish accord:* reference to the Anglo-Irish Agreement of 1985 giving the Republic of Ireland a consultative role in administering Northern Ireland (cf. "Info-Box", p. 67) **97–98** *resentment* [rɪˈzentmənt] (U): feeling of ill will or bitterness **107** *retribution* [ˌretrɪˈbjuːʃn] (U) (fml.): revenge, retaliation • *spark sth.* (infml.): be the immediate cause of sth., lead to sth. **110** *work odd jobs:* do small jobs of various kinds **113** *hearten sb.:* make sb. feel cheerful and encouraged **117** *be bent on sth.:* be determined on sth.

Talking about the text

1. What popular image has Belfast had to live with since the beginning of the Troubles?
2. How has the face of Belfast's inner city changed in the last few years?
3. What picture of Belfast city life on a weekday evening does the writer present?
4. What reminders are there that Belfast is the capital of a province torn by violence?
5. Describe the mood detected by the writer among the inhabitants of Belfast in his research for this article.

2

James Simmons
Claudy

In Northern Ireland, peaceful daily life can change rapidly, as the following poem illustrates.

A Ballad

The Sperrins surround it, the Faughan flows by,
at each end of Main Street, the hills and the sky,
the small town of Claudy at ease in the sun
last July in the morning, a new day begun.

How peaceful and pretty if the moment could stop.
McIlhenny is straightening things in his shop,
and his wife is outside serving petrol, and then,
a child takes a cloth to a big window-pane.

McCloskey is taking the weight off his feet,
and McClelland and Millar are sweeping the street,
and, delivering milk at the Beaufort Hotel,
young Temple's enjoying his first job quite well.

And Mrs McLaughlin is scrubbing her floor,
and Artie Hone's crossing the street to a door,
and Mrs Brown, looking around for her cat,
goes off up an entry – What's strange about that?

Not much – but before she comes back to the road
that strange car parked outside her door will explode,
and all of the people I've mentioned, outside,
will be waiting to die, or already have died.

An explosion too loud for your eardrums to bear,
and young children squealing like pigs in the square,
and all faces chalk white and streaked with bright red,
and the glass and the dust and the terrible dead ...

for an old lady's legs are ripped off, and the head
of a man's hanging open and still he's not dead.
He is screaming for mercy while his son stands and stares
and stares, and then, suddenly, quick, disappears.

And Christ! little Katharine Aikin is dead
and Mrs McCloskey is pierced through the head.
Meanwhile to Dungiven the killers have gone
and they're finding it hard to get through on the phone.

The Sperrins surround it, the Faughan flows by,
at each end of Main Street, the hills and the sky,
the small town of Claudy at ease in the sun
last July in the morning, a new day begun.

The Sperrin Mountains

Claudy [ˈklɔːdɪ]*:* small town in Co. Londonderry **2** *Sperrins* (pl.): mountains in Co. Londonderry • *Faughan* [fɔːn] **7** *straighten sth.* (infml.): tidy sth. **10** *take the weight off one's feet* (infml.): rest **17** *entry* (N.I.): narrow passage behind a row of terraced houses **32** *Dungiven* [– ˈ– –] **33** *get through on the phone:* (here) make a warning call to inform the general public of a planted bomb

Talking about the text

1. What kind of atmosphere is created in the first part of the poem?
2. How is the explosion described?
3. Explain the events related in the poem in the light of ll. 32–33.
4. Why does Simmons call the poem "A Ballad" (l. 1)?

3

John Pepper
It's No Use Talkin'

John Pepper has written numerous books on the English language as spoken in Northern Ireland. In the following excerpt from *See Me, See Her* (1978), a conversation between two women from Belfast talking about the difficulties of bringing up children serves as an example.

Just as it is possible to find a Yorkshireman (to say nothing of a Geordie) who will insist that their idiom can sometimes jar, so the speech of Northern Ireland has its critics.

These will include parents who prefer their children to be "well spoken", for example, besides teachers of English, and pedants.

The side you are on depends on whether you believe in rebuking a troublesome child with a restrained, "Would you please try and behave?" or favour roaring at them, "D'ye want me to draw my hand across yir gub?"

Take a doorstep conversation between two talkative Belfastwomen, Aggie and Bella. They are old friends. They are standing chatting at Aggie's front door, their arms folded. They are women with all the time in the world.

AGGIE: Ach, howerye Bella? It's nice to get a breath av air. I'm awful warm for I'm just aff the griddle.

BELLA: Right enough. It takes it outa ye.

AGGIE: See me? I don't mind the bakin' one bit. Made the wee lad a perr of trousers outa an oul perr of his da's and d'ye know, ye cudn't tell wherr he wiz comin' or goin'. I wuz nivver any use with a needle.

BELLA: Me nire. I cudn't make my wee Darathy a frack if ye wir to give me a medal. Headstrong wee article, mind ye. Wud drive ye up the walls.

AGGIE: Don't talk. I tole my wee lad if he didn't catch hisself on I'd give him a right skelp and what d'ye think he said? Said he go an' tell the battered babies people on me, so he did.

BELLA: It makes ye think.

AGGIE: Ach, ye cudn't tell him aught. I nearly give him the rounds of the kitchen.

BELLA: An' for why didden ye?

AGGIE: I toul him I'd tell his da. He'll murder ye, I toul him.

BELLA: That wud put him in his place.

AGGIE: Damn the put. The da has it in fer him anyway. He'll not miss him and hit the wall once he gets started.

BELLA: Childer! They're a handful.

AGGIE: Don't talk to me. Last week I found the wee whelp starin' inta the mare his da shaves in. I ast him what he was doin'. "Ye told me to watch myself, didden ye?" he says.

BELLA: There ye are ni.

AGGIE: Know what I'm goin' till tell ye? I usta think it wud be that nice if he was the kind of wee lad that wud chase butterflies. No fear. All he'll ivver chase after is an oul ball.

BELLA: Weans! All the same they can be the quare oul help when they like.

AGGIE: All the help they can be is to help ye spend yir money.

BELLA: It's no use talkin'.

AGGIE: Funny enough I was in the shap the orr day there and a woman beside me tole me she was havin' her sister's two wee girls for supper. Ye shudda seen the luck she got from the strange woman stannin' beside her. Honest to Gawd I believe the poor woman thought she was among a lock of cannibals.

BELLA: It makes ye think.

1 *Geordie* ['dʒɔːdɪ]: person from Newcastle in the north-east of England **2** *jar* (v.): have a harsh or unpleasant effect **3** *well spoken* (adj.): speaking correctly or in a refined way **5** *rebuke sb.* [rɪ'bjuːk]: express sharp or severe disapproval to sb.; reprove sb. **7** *gub* (N.I.): mouth **11–12** *I'm just aff the griddle* (N.I.): I have just finished baking **14** *see me?* (N.I.): do you know what I think? • *wee* (N.I. and Scot.): little **17** *frack* (N.I. pron.): frock **18** *headstrong:* determined; stubborn **19** *lad* (infml.): fellow • *catch oneself on* (non-standard): behave • *skelp* (n.) (N.I.): beating **20** *battered babies people* (infml.): (in Britain) Society for the Prevention of Cruelty to Children **23** *aught* (old use; N.I.): anything • *give sb. the rounds of sth.* (N.I.): chase and beat sb. around sth. (e.g. a room) **26** *put sb. in her or his place:* humiliate sb. who has been impertinent **27** *have it in fer sb.* (N.I. pron.) = *have it in for sb.* (infml.): intend to punish sb. **30** *whelp* (N.I.): badly-behaved child; rascal • *mare* (N.I. pron.): mirror **36** *wean* [wiːn] (N.I.): child • *the quare oul help* (N.I.): quite a help **39** *orr* (N.I. pron.): other **42** *lock* (N.I.): lot

Peaceful scene on Lough Neagh, the largest lake in the British Isles

INFO BOX

Ulster Speech

The language spoken in Northern Ireland today reflects some of the history of Ulster. Originally, the people of Ulster spoke Gaelic, a language very much different from English. Then, in the early 17th century, settlers arrived from Scotland and also from England. English became the dominant language in Northern Ireland, but it retained some of the qualities of the brand of language the early settlers had brought with them and incorporated certain elements of the Gaelic language (now very much diminished in Northern Ireland).

The three sources of modern-day Ulster speech are sometimes referred to by the national symbols of England, Scotland and Ireland – the rose, the thistle and the shamrock.

Elizabethan English:
The Brand of the Rose

Many examples of the English spoken in Queen Elizabeth I's reign can still be heard in every county in Northern Ireland. Thus, the word *heard* is often pronounced [hɪəd] rather than [hɜːd], and the Northern Irish pronunciation of *decent* is [deɪsnt], just as it generally was in Elizabethan England.

Lowland Scots:
The Brand of the Thistle

The north-east coast of Ireland was the main area of Scottish settlement in Ireland, and it is here that many Scottish speech features can still be found. The inhabitants of Ballymena (cf. map, p. 9), for instance, are often taken for Scots by people from outside Northern Ireland.

Ulster Gaelic:
The Brand of the Shamrock

The influence of the Gaelic language can still be noticed in some parts of Northern Ireland. Certain words which are in everyday use in Co. Antrim and in Co. Londonderry were adapted from Gaelic: a *shanty* (Gaelic *sean tigh* [ˌʃʌn ˈtiː]) is an old house, and when you hear somebody (not only in Northern Ireland, but also in England) speaking of "books (or people, whiskey etc.) *galore*", they are talking of "a lot of books", the original Gaelic expression *go leor* [gəˈlɔːr] meaning "enough".

4

Robert Johnstone

Observations across the Divide

Despite the Troubles, friendships between Northern Irish Protestants and Roman Catholics are possible and indeed quite normal among the well-educated middle class. In the following excerpt from his book *Images of Belfast* (1983), Protestant writer Robert Johnstone talks to his Catholic friend Liam.

Discussing with a friend the perils of being self-employed, we both decide it's better to be your own boss, despite the lack of unemployment benefit, occupational pension schemes and so on. We discover that neither of us is putting away money in an insurance plan for retirement. I offer a not entirely serious explanation: "After all, in thirty years' time we might be living in another country."

Liam agrees: "Yes, you never know. Even worse, we could be living in the same country."

"I remember," I say, "my father once told me he thought Northern Ireland had about another fifty years before it was reunited with the South."

"Before us Fenians outbred you, you mean."

"That, and I suppose also a gradual burying of hatchets. My dad thought the IRA were only putting off ..."

"The evil day?" asks Liam with a grin.

"No, not at all. I think he was probably as romantic about a united Ireland as any good republican. It was just that he didn't like to be pushed."

"Fifty years is a long time to wait."

"True, but I don't think he was necessarily unrealistic. We can be just as stubborn as you lot. You've kept it up for three hundred years. Anyway, what sort of country would it be that was reunited by force, with a million Prods as resentful and making as much trouble as half a million Catholics?"

Liam looks as if he is about to concede my point, reluctantly, but he's not finished yet: "Ireland, or the twenty-six counties, were liberated by force. Every country in the world has been freed or united by force. Can you think of one that wasn't?"

"Apart from St Kitts, not off hand. But do you really think the Provos are going to produce a free, happy and united Ireland in which all will be proud..."

I know I'm on safer ground here. Liam was active in the Civil Rights movement in the Sixties and his brother was briefly interned, one of the many harmless agitators Brian Faulkner and his security advisers could not distinguish from mad gunmen. But these days Liam shares my attitude, looking at the Provos' subsequent campaign with detachment and occasional disgust.

"A bunch of bloody lunatics" is his usual description of them, when he isn't trying to banter.

Eventually we agree that the Provos are prolonging the agony rather than ushering in a new dawn. In the meantime, as always, we go back to work like normal people, as if the whole world were not in a terrible state of chassis. (I often borrow that phrase from O'Casey to sum up our mutual resignation after such exchanges.)

Another time I asked Liam to tell me about his time in the Civil Rights. He tells it more as a series of funny stories than as the prologue to a revolution. As a schoolboy, I thought it was not only ideologically sound, but probably good fun as well. Liam confirms my assessment.

Those days are gone now. Liam stopped agitating and breaking the law when the agitators began to use gelignite and Co-op mixture. His only other demos were the early Peace People rallies. When he votes now, only once per election, he might vote for a different party than I would (though to be honest I never vote, as it only encourages the politicians), but I feel that between us we could work out a fairly reasonable system of power-sharing. Is Liam a typical Belfast Catholic? No more than I am a typical Protestant. In my more sensible moments I remember that there is no typical anything, only extraordinary individuals.

Although our attitudes and conclusions are so similar, I am occasionally shocked to be reminded of our differences. At election time, or during a moment of tension, Liam reveals the closeness of Catholic society: he will have heard through the grapevine what is likely to happen next, or what is the best method of tactical voting to keep out the Unionist. Catholic public opinion seems to form itself very quickly and, to an outsider, mysteriously. And sometimes Liam points out odd little distinctions: "Catholics wear discrimination like a badge, you know. They tell each other stories of how they've been discriminated against, almost as if it proves how Catholic they are." On the other hand he can be impatient with that attitude: "What's the point of feeling hard done-by? If you're looking for discrimination, you'll find it everywhere. Quite often it's just in the imagination."

I enjoy my apocalyptic conversations with Liam about politics. Our predicitions are just as unfettered as the alternate scenarios put forward by Conor Cruise O'Brien or Harold McCusker, though we cosily calculate the practical and personal details of each. In the "Swiss solution", for instance, with Northern Ireland divided into a myriad cantons, we wonder whether suspects would ever be extradited from the Falls to the Shankill. On repartition, I estimate which of my relations would be living in a foreign country if the border were moved to the River Bann. David, another friend, lays out his plan: "They can have Derry and South Armagh so long as we – whoever 'we' are – can keep the Antrim coast."

"Actually, it doesn't say much for the power of prayer that the Pope is still alive and kicking."

"What about Lough Erne?"

He begins to look dubious. "Yes. And it would be a pity to lose the Sperrins."

"Forget the Sperrins, keep Strangford. And South Armagh is rather pretty when the sun shines."

"Aye, but you don't want to be greedy. Maybe we could lease them back, like the New Territories round Hong Kong. Just for the summer holidays."

How pleasant it is to imagine fantastic new countries with fantastic new political structures. One of our favourite fantasies is an independent Ulster, with Ian Paisley as President. But we decide we probably wouldn't like it.

"There'd be no swings on Sunday."

"And no drink the rest of the week."

"No X films."

"No *Sound of Music* – there's nuns in that."

"I suppose it can't be all bad."

"No sex please, we're Protestant."

"There'd be no EEC, and certainly *no* Treaty of Rome."

"But to prove that Ulster was a part of the international community, we could host the Olympic Games ..."

"Athletics at the Mary Peters Track."

"Tractor-backing at Greenmount."

"Olympic Bible-thumping at Ballymena."

"Throwing Catholics to the lions at the Antrim Forum."

The stranger from England, no doubt delighted to find an example of Protestant and Catholic living in harmony, stands aghast when Liam and I taunt each other in fun about religion. The opportunities are manifold. They can begin with a crack about the Catholic birth-rate and usually end up with the sentiment that Protestants should go back to where they came from and leave Ireland to the Irish. Perhaps it sounds a bit hair-raising to our well-meaning guest, but with us it is a mark of affection. We may sneakingly believe there is a nugget of truth in the stereotypes – that Protestants are hard-working, conscientious, unimaginative or whatever – but the prejudices and public rhetoric really have no more meaning than a continuous programme of fantasy films.

1 *peril* (C): dangerous thing or circumstance **6** *Liam* [ˈlɪəm] **10** *Fenian* [ˈfiːnjən]: member of a 19th century Irish nationalist organization; (here) Irish Catholic • *outbreed sb.* (infml.): gradually outnumber sb. **11** *hatchet:* (hier) Kriegsbeil **12** *put sth. off:* postpone sth., delay sth. **19** *Prod* (N.I. infml.): Protestant • *resentful* [rɪˈzentfl]: feeling bitter or angry **21** *concede sth.:* admit that sth. is true **22** *the twenty-six counties* (infml.): Republic of Ireland **24** *St Kitts = Federation of Saint Christopher and Nevis:* island group in the Caribbean Sea formerly under British rule, which gained full independence in 1983 • *Provos* (abbr.) = *Provisional Irish Republican Army:* militant organization of Irish nationalists (cf. "Info-Box", p. 23) **26** *Civil Rights movement:* (here) movement against discrimination of Northern Irish Catholics (cf. "Info-Box", p. 22) **27** *intern sb.* [ɪnˈtɜːn ☆ -ˈtɜːrn]: put sb. in prison without trial **27–28** *Brian Faulkner* [ˈfɔːknə] (1921–1977): last prime minister of Northern Ireland (1973–1974), responsible for the policy of internment (cf. l. 27) **29** *subsequent:* later, following **30** *detachment* (U): indifference, lack of emotion **31** *lunatic* [ˈluːnətɪk] (derog.): insane and irresponsible person **32** *banter:* speak playfully or jokingly **33** *usher sth. in* (fig.): mark the beginning of sth. **35** *chassis* [ˈʃæsɪ ☆ -siː]: body of a car; word used by a character in Sean O'Casey's (cf. l. 36) play *Juno and the Paycock* (1925) to mean "chaos" **36** *O'Casey = Sean O'Casey* (1884–1964): Irish dramatist • *mutual* [ˈmjuːtʃuəl] (infml.): shared by two or more people **42** *gelignite* [ˈdʒelɪgnaɪt]: powerful explosive • *Co-op mixture:* home-made explosive **43** *Peace People:* Northern Irish peace movement formed in 1976 by Betty Williams and Máiread Corrigan and supported by people of all faiths (cf. "Info-Box", p. 22) • *rally:* large gathering of people with a common (usu. political) purpose • *only once per election:* reference to the former Northern Irish practice of allowing prosperous businessmen (usu. Protestants) more than one vote in an election **51** *hear sth. through the grapevine* (fig.): hear sth. (news) from another person **52** *tactical voting:* practice of voting not for the candidate or party one prefers but for another that is more likely to defeat the candidate one wishes to be defeated **53** *Unionist:* member of the Ulster Unionist Party or the Democratic Unionist Party (cf. "Info-Box", p. 23) **57** *hard done-by* (infml.): unfairly treated **61** *unfettered* (adj.): free, unhindered · *Conor Cruise O'Brien* (1917–): Southern Irish historian, politician and journalist **62** *Harold McCusker* (1940–): Northern Irish politician; deputy leader of the Ulster Unionist Party since 1982 **63** *myriad* ['mɪrɪəd]: extremely large number **64** *extradite sb.* ['– – –]: send sb. to a country where they are wanted for trial · *Falls:* Catholic area in Belfast **65** *Shankill:* Protestant area in Belfast · *repartition:* new drawing of borders **66** *River Bann:* river dividing the counties Londonderry and Antrim **67** *Armagh* [ɑː'mɑː] **71** *Sperrins* (pl.): mountains in Co. Londonderry **72** *Strangford:* arm of the sea on the eastern coast of Northern Ireland **82** *Ian Paisley* (1926–): extreme right wing Protestant clergyman in Northern Ireland (cf. "Info-Box", p. 23) **85** *no swings on Sunday:* reference to the belief of some Protestants that children should not be allowed to play on Sundays **87** *X film:* film for adults only **88** *"Sound of Music":* popular US film of 1965 **90** *No sex please, we're Protestant:* reference to the comedy *No Sex Please, We're British* (1975) **91** *Treaty of Rome:* founding document of the European Community, signed in 1957 **94** *Mary Peters Track:* athletics stadium in Belfast, named after a Belfast athlete **95** *Greenmount:* agricultural college in Northern Ireland **96** *Ballymena* [bælɪ'miːnə]: town in Northern Ireland where Ian Paisley's (cf. l. 82) church is located **97** *Antrim Forum:* leisure centre in the town of Antrim **99** *aghast* [– '–]: filled with horror or amazement · *taunt sb.* [tɔːnt]: try to provoke sb. with critical remarks **100** *crack* (n.) (infml.): joke **103** *sneaking* (adj.): secret and unexpressed **104** *nugget* (fig.): small amount **105** *conscientious* [ˌkɒnʃɪ'enʃəs ☆ ˌkɑːn-]: gewissenhaft

Talking about the text

1. What is the writer's and Liam's general attitude towards violence as an instrument for bringing about political change?
2. Describe how Liam's attitude to the Troubles has changed since the sixties.
3. How would you characterize Johnstone's, Liam's and David's (cf. l. 66) view of the future of Northern Ireland?
4. To what extent could the relationship between Robert Johnstone and his friend Liam serve as a model for Northern Irish society?
5. Summarize and comment on the author's opinion about stereotypes.

CHAPTER IV

Poets and Writers

1

JOHN HEWITT

Once Alien Here

In Northern Ireland, different cultures and languages met – or clashed. John Hewitt reflects on the consequences this has for himself and for his poetry.

John Hewitt

Once alien here my fathers built their house,
claimed, drained, and gave the land the shapes of use,
and for their urgent labour grudged no more
than shuffled pennies from the hoarded store
of well rubbed words that had left their overtones
in the ripe England of the mounded downs.

The sullen Irish limping to the hills
bore with them the enchantments and the spells
that in the clans' free days hung gay and rich
on every twig of every thorny hedge,
and gave the rain-pocked stone a meaning past
the blurred engraving of the fibrous frost.

So I, because of all the buried men
in Ulster clay, because of rock and glen
and mist and cloud and quality of air
as native in my thought as any here,
who now would seek a native mode to tell
our stubborn wisdom individual,

yet lacking skill in either scale of song,
the graver English, lyric Irish tongue,
must let this rich earth so enhance the blood
with steady pulse where now is plunging mood
till thought and image may, identified,
find easy voice to utter each aright.

alien ['eɪlɪən] (adj.): foreign **3** *grudge sth.* [grʌdʒ]: do or give sth. very unwillingly **4** *shuffle sth.:* move sth. around to different positions • *hoard sth.* [hɔːd ☆ hɔːrd]: carefully collect and guard sth. **6** *mounded* (adj.): hilly • *downs:* (pl.): area of open rolling land, especially in the south of England **7** *sullen*: silent, bad-tempered and gloomy • *limp* (v.): hinken **8** *enchantment:* Verzauberung • *spell:* Zauberspruch **9** *clan:* (in medieval Ireland) group of families descended from a common ancestor **11** *rain-pocked* (adj.): having holes or depressions in the surface caused by the rain • *past:* beyond the limits of sth.; (here) deeper than sth. **12** *blurred* (adj.): unclear, indistinct • *engraving:* (Kupfer-, Stahl-) Stich • *fibrous* ['faɪbrəs]: faserig **14** *clay* (U): Ton, Lehm • *glen:* narrow valley **17** *mode:* way or manner in which something is done **18** *stubborn* ['stʌbən ☆ -bərn]: strong-willed, determined not to give way **19** *scale:* Tonleiter **20** *grave:* serious **21** *enhance sb./sth.* [ɪn'hɑːns ☆ -'hæns]: increase the good qualities of sb./sth. **22** *plunge:* fall suddenly with force **24** *utter sth.:* say or speak sth. • *aright* (adv.) (lit.): rightly

Talking about the text

1. Who were the poet's "fathers" (l. 1) and why are they said to have been alien?
2. Which language is referred to in ll. 3–6 and how is it described?
3. What does the poet tell us about the native inhabitants of the country?
4. How does the poet see his own position with regard to Ulster and with regard to his poetry?

A centre of art and entertainment: Belfast's Grand Opera

INFO BOX

Northern Ireland – The Literary Scene

Politics, some would say, is the death of literature. Troubled times and civil unrest may produce writers with a cause and volumes of protest poetry, but very little literature of real lasting value.

If this is true, Northern Ireland is an exception. In the past 20 or 30 years the province has seen an astonishing blossoming of literature, a phenomenon sometimes referred to as the "Ulster Renaissance". Today the Northern Irish literary scene boasts a greater number of poets, dramatists and fiction writers with an international reputation than one would expect from such a troubled and relatively small region.

Among the writers of fiction, the most important is probably Bernard MacLaverty, known for his best-selling novel *Cal* (1983) and for his short stories (cf. Ch. IV, Text 2).

Plays written by Northern Irish dramatists are not only successful in Ulster and in the Republic of Ireland, but also in England and elsewhere. Brian Friel treats the themes of exile and Irish identity. He is the co-founder of the Field Day Theatre Company, which since 1980 has produced plays by Northern Irish authors such as Tom Paulin, Thomas Kilroy and others. Anne Devlin has written both for the stage and for television (cf. Ch. IV, Text 4).

It is in the field of poetry that the Ulster Renaissance has produced the richest and most original literature. Seamus Heaney is considered by many to be one of the most important living poets in the English language (cf. Ch. IV, Text 5). Other poets who have won international acclaim are Derek Mahon, Michael Longley, Medbh [meɪv] McGuckian and Paul Muldoon.

The contemporary literary scene in Northern Ireland goes back to the 1947 Education Act, which guaranteed free education to Catholic and Protestant children alike. As a result, the Catholic population of Ulster found its tongue. This may have led to the beginnings of the civil unrest in the late 1960s as well as to the emergence of modern Northern Irish literature.

Today's writers and poets rarely deal directly with the Troubles, although the political situation is often reflected in their writings. Much of Northern Irish literature tries to overcome sectarianism by transcending the conflict between Catholics and Protestants. As poet Derek Mahon says: "The function of the arts is not to change maps but to change the expressions on the faces of men and women."

2

Bernard MacLaverty
Father and Son

Personal relationships are rarely immune to the conflicts that tear society, as the following short story illustrates.

Because I do not sleep well I hear my father rising to go to work. I know that in a few minutes he will come in to look at me sleeping. He will want to check that I came home last night. He will stand in his bare feet, his shoes and socks in his hand, looking at me. I will sleep for him. Downstairs I hear the snap of the switch on the kettle. I hear him not eating anything, going about the kitchen with a stomach full of wind. He will come again to look at me before he goes out to his work. He will want a conversation. He climbs the stairs and stands breathing through his nose with an empty lunch box in the crook of his arm, looking at me.

This is my son who let me down. I love him so much it hurts but he won't talk to me. He tells me nothing. I hear him groan and see his eyes flicker open. When he sees me he turns away, a heave of bedclothes in his wake.

"Wake up, son. I'm away to my work. Where are you going today?"
"What's it to you?"
"If I know what you're doing I don't worry as much."
"Shit."

I do not sleep. My father does not sleep. The sound of ambulances criss-crosses the dark. I sleep with the daylight. It is safe. At night I hear his bare feet click as he lifts them, walking the lino. The front door shudders as he leaves.

My son is breaking my heart. It is already broken. Is it my fault there is no woman in the house? Is it my fault a good woman should die? His face was never softer than when after I had shaved. A baby pressed to my shaved cheek. Now his chin is sandpaper. He is a man. When he was a boy I took him fishing. I taught him how to tie a blood-knot, how to cast a fly, how to strike so the fish would not escape. How to play a fish. The green bus to quiet days in Toome. Him pestering me with questions. If I leave him alone he will break my heart anyway. I must speak to him. Tonight at tea. If he is in.

"You should be in your bed. A man of your age. It's past one."
"Let me make you some tea."
The boy shrugs and sits down. He takes up the paper between him and his father.
"What do you be doing out to this time?"
"Not again."
"Answer me."
"Talking."
"Who with?"
"Friends. Just go to bed, Da, will you?"

"What do you talk about?"
"Nothing much."
"Talk to me, son."
"What about?"

My son, he looks confused. I want you to talk to me the way I hear you talk to people at the door. I want to hear you laugh with me like you used to. I want to know what you think. I want to know why you do not eat more. No more than pickings for four weeks. Your face is thin. Your fingers, orange with nicotine. I pulled you away from death once and now you will not talk to me. I want to know if you are in danger again.

"About..."
"You haven't shaved yet."
"I'm just going to. The water in the kettle is hot."
"Why do you shave at night?"
"Because in the morning my hand shakes."

Your hand shakes in the morning, Da, because you're a coward. You think the world is waiting round the corner to blow your head off. A breakfast of two Valium and the rest of them rattling in your pocket, walking down the street to your work. Won't answer the door without looking out the bedroom window first. He's scared of his own shadow.

Son, you are living on borrowed time. Your hand shook when you got home. I have given you the life you now have. I fed you soup from a spoon when your own hand would have spilled it. Let me put my arm around your shoulders and let me listen to what is making you thin. At the weekend I will talk to him.

It is hard to tell if his bed has been slept in. It is always rumpled. I have not seen my son for two days. Then, on the radio, I hear he is dead. They give out his description. I drink milk. I cry.
But he comes in for his tea.

"Why don't you tell me where you are?"
"Because I never know where I am."

My mother is dead but I have another one in her place. He is an old woman. He has been crying. I know he prays for me all the time. He used to dig the garden, grow vegetables and flowers for half the street. He used to fish. To take me fishing. Now he just waits. He sits and waits for me and the weeds have taken over. I would like to slap his face and make a man out of him.

"I let you go once – and look what happened."
"Not this again."
The boy curls his lip as if snagged on a fish-hook.

For two years I never heard a scrape from you. I read of London in the papers. Watched scenes from London on the news, looking over the reporter's shoulder at people walking in the street. I know you, son, you are easily led. Then a doctor phoned for me at work. The poshest man I ever spoke to.

"I had to go and collect you. Like a dog."

The boy had taken up a paper. He turns the pages noisily, crackling like fire.

"A new rig-out from Littlewoods."

Socks, drawers, shirt, the lot. In a carrier bag. The doctor said he had to burn what was on you. I made you have your girl's hair cut. It was Belfast before we spoke. You had the taint of England in your voice.

"Today I thought you were dead."

Every day you think I am dead. You live in fear. Of your own death. Peeping behind the curtains, the radio always loud enough to drown any noise that might frighten you, double locking doors. When you think I am not looking you hold your stomach. You undress in the dark for fear of your shadow falling on the window-blind. At night you lie with the pillow over your head. By your bed a hatchet which you pretend to have forgotten to tidy away. Mice have more courage.

"Well I'm not dead."

"Why don't you tell me where you go?"

"Look, Da, I have not touched the stuff since I came back. Right?"

"Why don't you have a girl like everybody else?"

"Oh fuck."

He bundles the paper and hurls it in the corner and stamps up the stairs to his room. The old man shouts at the closed door.

"Go and wash your mouth out."

He cries again, staring at the ceiling so that the tears run down his ears.

My son, he is full of hatred. For me, for everything. He spits when he speaks. When he shouts his voice breaks high and he is like a woman. He grinds his teeth and his skin goes white about his mouth. His hands shake. All because I ask him where he goes. Perhaps I need to show him more love. Care for him more than I do.

I mount the stairs quietly to apologise. My son, I am sorry. I do it because I love you. Let me put my arm around you and talk like we used to on the bus from Toome. Why do you fight away from me?

The door swings open and he pushes a hand-gun beneath the pillow. Seen long enough, black and squat, dull like a garden slug. He sits, my son, his hands idling empty, staring hatred.

"Why do you always spy on me, you nosey old bastard?" His voice breaks, his eyes bulge.

"What's that? Under your pillow?"

"It's none of your fucking business."

He kicks the door closed in my face with his bare foot.

I am in the dark of the landing. I must pray for him. On my bended knees I will pray for him to be safe. Perhaps I did not see what I saw. Maybe I am mistaken. My son rides pillion on a motor-bike. Tonight I will not sleep. I do not think I will sleep again.

It's ten o'clock. The news begins. Like a woman I stand drying a plate, watching the headlines. There is a ring at the door. The boy answers it, his shirt-tail out. Voices in the hallway.
My son with friends. Talking. What he does not do with me.

There is a bang. A dish-cloth drops from my hand and I run to the kitchen door. Not believing, I look into the hallway. There is a strange smell. My son is lying on the floor, his head on the bottom stair, his feet on the threshold. The news has come to my door. The house is open to the night. There is no one else. I go to him with damp hands.

"Are you hurt?"

Blood is spilling from his nose.

They have punched you and you are not badly hurt. Your nose is bleeding. Something cold at the back of your neck.

I take my son's limp head in my hands and see a hole in his nose that should not be there. At the base of the nostril.

My son, let me put my arms around you.

7 *crook:* bend, curve **9** *let sb. down:* disappoint sb. **11** *heave* (n.): (here) pile • *in sb.'s wake:* coming after or following sb. **18** *lino* (infml.): linoleum **22** *blood-knot:* special fisherman's knot **22–23** *cast a fly:* throw a fishing line with a (natural or artificial) fly on the hook **23** *play sth.:* allow sth. (a fish) to exhaust itself by pulling against the line **24** *Toome:* small town on the northern shore of Lough Neagh [ˌlɒx ˈneɪ] • *pester sb.:* annoy sb. **29** *What do you be doing?* (N.I.): What are you doing? **41** *pickings* (pl.): very small portions of food **59** *rumple sth.:* make sth. untidy **68** *weed:* Unkraut **73** *scrape* (n.) (N.I. infml.): little bit **75** *lead sb.:* influence sb. **76** *posh* (adj.) (infml.): upper-class **79** *rig-out* (BE infml.): outfit of clothes • *Littlewoods:* name of a British chain of stores **80** *drawers* (pl.) (old-fashioned): underpants **82** *taint* (n.): trace of some bad quality **84** *peep:* look cautiously **88** *hatchet* [ˈhætʃɪt]: axe **107** *squat* [skwɒt] (adj.): short and thick • *dull:* not bright • *slug:* snail with no shell • *idle* (v.): do nothing **110** *bulge:* swell outward **115** *ride pillion:* ride on the passenger seat of a motorcycle **130** *limp:* not firm

Talking about the text

1. What indications are there in the text that the story is set in Northern Ireland and what can you conclude about the son's activities?
2. Analyze the significance of the text's structure.
3. Describe the son's feelings towards his father.
4. What did their relationship use to be like and why did it change?
5. To what extent do the father's worries apply more aptly to himself than to his son?

3

Donna Foote, David Lehman

Resolving the Tensions

In the last few decades, Northern Ireland has seen a remarkable renaissance in the arts, especially in literature. Poets like Seamus Heaney, Paul Muldoon and Derek Mahon as well as playwrights like Brian Friel have become internationally known.
The following excerpt from an article in an American news magazine looks at the beginnings of this development and at today's literary scene.

It all started 23 years ago in a flat in Belfast's Fitzwilliam Street where the English poet Philip Hobsbaum, then a lecturer at Queen's University, assembled the circle of young writers that came to be known as The Group. "What we're seeing is the fallout from the original explosion," says critic Edna Longley, a graduate of The Group. A piece of enlightened social legislation – the 1947 Education Act, which guaranteed free education to Catholic and Protestant children alike – had a lot to do with the release of this literary energy. It was under this act that Ulster's Catholic population, its silent minority, found its tongue and began to air its grievances. The evolution of the province's civil-rights movement in the '60s can be traced directly to 1947. The same may be true, alas, of the violence. Heaney owns up to his early ambivalence about the Troubles: "The moral sense said, 'This is awful.' The imagination said, 'Jesus, this is what I've been waiting for'."

Indelible snapshots: The relationship between the literary revival and the political tumult is nothing if not complex. As Dillon Johnston points out in his excellent book *Irish Poetry After Joyce*, with few exceptions the poets of Northern Ireland treat the Troubles obliquely. Lyrical by intent and elegiac by mood, they are masters of indirection, refusing to editorialize about the indelible snapshots of violence that they present.

Heaney's work is more forthright than most. In such poems as "Act of Union", he personifies England as an "imperially male" aggressor and Ireland as a ruined maid. Yet Heaney quite often invokes such highly charged allegories only to veer away from the political implications; he flashes "semaphores of hurt." This tendency is the more pronounced in Muldoon's poems with their multiple ironies. Being a spokesman for a cause is the last thing on Muldoon's mind – or on Mahon's. "The function of the arts," Mahon says, "is not to change maps but to change the expressions on the faces of men and women." Or, as Heaney puts it, defending a poetry of indirection, "It isn't the business of the germ to explain but to get on with the disease."

Ulster is, of course, both British and Irish. "Everyone in Northern Ireland lives in two places at once," says Heaney. In a number of cases that's quite literally true; Irish writers have a history of physically uprooting themselves from the homes they can't spiritually escape. Muldoon, until recently a BBC producer in Belfast, will take up a teaching post at Cambridge University in the fall. Heaney divides his year between Dublin and Harvard University. For Mahon, who currently lives in Dublin, the theme of dislocation is central. In poem after poem, Mahon depicts a divided speaker, in self-imposed exile from the "barbarous" and "fire-loving" North yet desperately homesick for it as well. The image of a deserted garage becomes Mahon's unlikely trope for home: "But the cracked panes reveal a dark/Interior echoing with the cries of children" who left long ago.

Study in betrayal: Where the resolutely private Medbh McGuckian is reluctant to tackle the Troubles head-on, the Field Day Theatre Company feeds off the opposite impulse. Founded in Londonderry six years ago by playwright Friel and actor Stephen Rea, Field Day – a pun on the founders' name – has put on a play a year since its première production of Friel's brilliant *Translations* in 1980. It also publishes a series of provocative pamphlets intended to explore the intersection of culture and politics. Tom Paulin, perhaps the most aggressively political of the Ulster poets, has pamphleteered in favor of *A Dictionary of Irish English* – and adapted *Antigone* to fit the particulars of Northern Ireland in his play, *The Riot Act.* The company's production of Thomas Kilroy's new play *Double Cross*, a study in betrayal during World War II, is playing to packed houses as it crisscrosses Ireland. It's slated to start a London run this month.

Field Day's board of directors consists of three men from the Catholic tradition and three from the Protestant, a fact that signals a hopeful truth about the artistic community in Ulster: it has strived to transcend sectarian differences, not simply wish them away. The people of Northern Ireland have had little enough to cheer about in recent years. The clash between Unionists and Nationalists, between the orange and the green, admits of no easy solutions, and a violent stalemate seems likely to continue. That so much creative and intellectual activity has flourished against so violent a backdrop is itself a triumph of the imagination. "When the psyche is attracted to two opposing commands, it resolves the conflict symbolically," says Heaney in what could serve as the credo to the Ulster poets. "Art is the dancing place where the tensions are resolved."

Seamus Heaney [ˌʃeɪməs 'hiːnɪ] • *Muldoon* [– '–] • *Mahon* ['mɑːhən] • *Friel* [friːl] **8** *graduate* ['grædʒʊət] (n.): Absolvent/in **9** *enlightened* (adj.): free from prejudice **16** *air one's grievances* ['griːvənsɪz]: talk about one's causes for complaint or protest **19** *alas* [ə'læs] (interj.) (lit.): expressing sorrow or regret **20** *own up to sth.:* admit sth. **25** *indelible* [ɪn'deləbl]: unauslöschlich **31** *oblique* [ə'bliːk] (adj.): indirect **32** *elegiac* [ˌelɪ'dʒaɪək] (adj.) (fml.): mournful; expressing sorrow **33–34** *editorialize* [ˌ– – '– – – –] (AE): express an opinion (as in a newspaper editorial) **40** *invoke sth.* (fml.): etwas heraufbeschwören **41–42** *veer away from sb./sth.:* (here) move suddenly away from sb./sth.; avoid sb./sth. **43** *semaphore:* (here) message **53** *germ:* bacterium **73** *trope* [trəʊp] (fml.): figurative use of a word or a phrase **78** *Medbh* [meɪv] **79** *tackle sth. head-on:* deal with sth. (e.g. a problem) without trying to avoid it **91** *pamphleteer* [ˌ– – '–]: distribute leaflets **93** *"Antigone":* tragedy by the ancient Greek dramatist Sophocles **99** *slate sth.* (AE infml.): plan that sth. will happen at a specified time **109–110** *the orange and the green:* (in Northern Ireland) colours symbolizing (Protestant) Unionists and (Catholic) Nationalists **111** *stalemate:* Stillstand; Sackgasse **114** *backdrop* (AE) = (BE) *backcloth* (fig.): background

Talking about the text

1. What lay behind the revival of literature that occurred in Northern Ireland in the 1960s?
2. Explain in your own words Seamus Heaney's early ambivalence about the Troubles (cf. ll. 21–24)?

3. What is the attitude of the poets quoted in the article to the conflict in Northern Ireland?
4. Explain and comment on Heaney's statement quoted in ll. 115–121.
5. Find out more about the ancient Greek tragedy *Antigone* and suggest how one might apply it to the Northern Irish situation.

4

ANNE DEVLIN
Loyalties

Politics and private lives interlock in the following excerpt from Anne Devlin's television play *The Long March* (1986). Helen Walsh has just left her husband Cliff and her home in England and has returned to her native Belfast, where she is now doing research for her friend Fergus Sloan, who is writing a book on the Northern Irish prison system. Helen's father Joe is a prominent Catholic trade unionist and city councillor. Her mother Rose is busy preparing the forthcoming wedding of Helen's sister.

[Int. The WALSHES' living room. Falls Road. West Belfast. Evening. 9.00pm. *JOE WALSH is sitting at his work table in the bay window of the living room; he is finishing a piece of correspondence. HELEN is sitting on the sofa surrounded by her work for FERGUS: copies of law reports. She is reading the evening* Belfast Telegraph. *JOE gets up to look for a container for the paper he has been writing on. He can't resist looking at the papers around HELEN. He is curious about her work. ROSE is at the dining-room table with her seating arrangement for the wedding. Time: 9 April 1979.]*

HELEN *[Putting down the paper, to JOE]:* Some group calling itself the Irish National Liberation Army has claimed responsibility for Neave's murder.

ROSE *[To JOE]:* The Sullivans can't come. That means we can ask Jim Quinn and Liam Brady.

HELEN: Irish National Liberation Army? Who are they?

JOE: They're a breakaway group from the Officials.

ROSE: Joe!

HELEN: The Official IRA are socialists. Are the INLA?

JOE: That crowd? The only socialism the INLA recognize is national socialism!

ROSE: Joe! Did you hear me? We can ask Jim Quinn and Liam Brady. The only trouble is they're widowers. *[JOE is looking blank.]* Could we put them on the same table or would that be too morbid? What do you think?

Joe: Put what on the same table?

Rose: Jim Quinn and Liam Brady.

Joe: Rose, what are we talking about?

Rose: Oh for God's sake, Joe. Would you ever listen to me. The wedding. Can we put Jim and Liam on the same table at the reception. Or would they just talk about their wives?

Joe: You know best, Rose. You do what you like.

Rose *[Hurt]:* I was only asking. *[She gets up from the table and goes to the kitchen.]* I'm sorry to have interrupted your intellectual conversation.

Joe *[Sighs. He sits down beside* Helen.*]:* Your mammy says you're working for Fergus Sloan. He's doing a book?

Relatives of H-Block hunger strikers hold a vigil (1980)

Helen: On punishment. He's looking at the prison system. He's also writing a pamphlet on the H-Block protest. I'm supposed to be setting up the interviews in Andersonstown. I had to see Frank Molloy today. He sends his regards.

Joe *[Stubbornly]:* The Molloys are Provos.

Helen *[Shocked]:* They're still people. Ordinary human beings like you and me. *[Quotes]* "I am human. I count nothing human alien to me."

Joe *[Gets up from beside her immediately.]:* Oh Jesus. You've been away a long time. All we need is you to come back and tell us how to behave.

Helen *[Nervously]:* I don't know what to say. You asked me what I was doing and I told you. You dismiss it. I defend it. What do you expect me to do?

Joe: I don't expect you to come back here and work for the Provos!

Helen: Daddy, what's happening in the Maze affects everybody.

Joe: Fergus Sloan walks past me in the street.

HELEN: You always do this to me. You always confront me with loyalties. You or Fergus. You or Cliff. You or –

JOE *[Furious, gets to his feet.]:* Is that so?

HELEN *[Quickly gets to her feet.]:* Yes it is so!

JOE: I'm to blame for your marriage failure!

HELEN: I didn't say that. God Almighty, I wish you and my mother would stop using the word failure about me.

JOE: What word would you like me to use? Success?

HELEN: Look Daddy. I played it all the way along the line your way. I went to university. I did a law degree. I didn't go to art college.

JOE: You went to a university but sure you threw it all away when you went to work in the library. A librarian! What kind of satisfaction is that for anyone. Have you no responsibility for what you owe the people who fought for your right to an education? I don't see you coming to work for the Trade Unions! I don't see you giving the Labour Movement anything back.

*[*ROSE *comes out of the kitchen.]*

ROSE: For God's sake, are you two at it again? You know what's wrong with you, Joe, she's too like you.

JOE: If I'd had half her chances I'd have made something of myself by now. *[To* HELEN*]* I left school at eleven.

HELEN: You can't blame me for that!

JOE: And that was staying on longer than anybody else in the street because the parish priest persuaded my mother to send me back for another year to keep the attendance numbers up so that the schoolmaster could get his salary.

HELEN: It happened to you, not to me. It happened to you! *[Focus on* HELEN*'s face.]*

JOE: You can't say that. Listen to me: my family came from the country to the city for work – from the wheat fields to the flour mills. I grew up as a barefoot boy in the Falls. I sold sticks – firewood – for money. From the orange-boxes that the greengrocer left in the entry. I didn't get my first pair of boots until I joined the Fianne. It was part of the uniform. I also got my first coat that way: a long green coat. And the Fianne ran the history classes at night. I was interned when I was seventeen and I read Kier Hardie in prison. When I came out I was a socialist. *[Joe turns away from her, and goes to his wife who is sitting nervously by the table. He sits, while he continues.]* You didn't have to join the IRA to get an education or boots or a coat – a Labour government in England saved you from that fate. A welfare state and a new Education Act. So you can't say it hasn't happened to you.

HELEN *[Following him across the room]:* When I first went into grammar school and I came home with a copy of *Macbeth* in my schoolbag, I was so excited I showed it to you. And you said: "I read that in prison." You've never let me forget what I owe. You want me to be somebody else. You always have. *[She is nearly in tears.]*

JOE: That's a damn lie! *[He gets to his feet again.]*

ROSE: Oh stop this, please. Everybody's fighting at the moment. I'm sick of it. I want a quiet house. *[*HELEN *walks away across the room.]*

JOE: Have you made your mind up whether you're going or staying here yet?

HELEN: Yes. I'm moving tomorrow. Michael's flat is empty while he's in Dublin on sabbatical. He wants me to keep an eye on the place for him.

JOE: Where's his flat?

HELEN: Stranmillis.

Joe *[A last thrust]:* Oh aye. I didn't expect it would be in the Falls.

[She quickly picks up all her papers.]

Helen: I'll leave my phone number in case you want to ring me.

[She goes to leave the room.]

Rose: You'll be coming to the wedding?

Helen: I don't know. The last thing I feel like at the moment is a wedding.

*[*Helen *leaves.* Rose *turns to* Joe *bewildered.]*

1 *Int.* (abbr.) = *interior* • *Falls Road:* road in a Catholic area of Belfast (cf. map on p. 14) **9** *Neave* = *Airey Neave* [niːv] (1916–1979): Conservative MP and shadow Northern Ireland Secretary of State, who was killed in the car park of the Houses of Parliament in Westminster **10** *Liam* ['lɪəm] **18** *blank* (adj.): without expression, understanding or interest **30** *pamphlet* ['– –]: booklet expressing a political opinion **31** *H-Block protest:* protest action by Catholic political prisoners held in an H-shaped cell block of the Maze Prison at Long Kesh, Northern Ireland, from 1975 (cf. "Info-Box", p. 22) **32** *Andersonstown:* Catholic suburb of Belfast, renowned for Provisional IRA activity (cf. map on p. 14) **33** *Provo* (infml.): member of the Provisional IRA (cf. "Info-Box", p. 23) **35** *"I am human. I count nothing human alien to me":* quotation from the ancient Roman poet Terence **41** *Maze* = *Maze Prison* (cf. l. 31) **44** *Cliff:* in the play, Helen's husband **69** *Falls:* Catholic, predominantly working-class area of Belfast (cf. map on p. 14) **71** *Fianne* [fɪ'ʌnə] (Irish): soldiers; (here) the IRA **73** *intern sb.* [– '–]: put sb. in prison without trial • *Kier Hardie* = *James Kier Hardie* ['kɪə 'hɑːdɪ] (1856–1915): British Labour leader **77** *Education Act:* act of 1947, which gave Catholic and Protestant children alike the right of free education **80** *"Macbeth":* drama by William Shakespeare (1564–1616) **88** *sabbatical* (n.): leave given at intervals to university teachers for travel or study **90** *Stranmillis:* university area of Belfast (cf. map on p. 14) **91** *aye* [aɪ] (interj.) (N.I.): yes

Talking about the text

1. What is Joe's opinion of his daughter Helen?
2. What factors formed Joe's political way of thinking?
3. Comparing Joe and Helen, what similarities and what differences can you see?
4. Describe the position Helen's mother holds in this scene.

5

Seamus Heaney
Digging

In the following poem Seamus Heaney thinks about his father and his grandfather. Remembering the past, he compares their work with his own.

Between my finger and my thumb
The squat pen rests; snug as a gun.

Under my window, a clean rasping sound
When the spade sinks into gravelly ground:
My father, digging. I look down

Till his straining rump among the flowerbeds
bends low, comes up twenty years away
Stooping in rhythm through potato drills
Where he was digging.

The coarse boot nestled on the lug, the shaft
Against the inside knee was levered firmly.
He rooted out tall tops, buried the bright edge deep
To scatter new potatoes that we picked
Loving their cool hardness in our hands.

By God, the old man could handle a spade.
Just like his old man.

My grandfather cut more turf in a day
Than any other man on Toner's bog.
Once I carried him milk in a bottle
Corked sloppily with paper. He straightened up
To drink it, then fell to right away

Nicking and slicing neatly, heaving sods
Over his shoulder, going down and down
For the good turf. Digging.

The cold smell of potato mould, the squelch and slap
Of soggy peat, the curt cuts of an edge
Through living roots awaken in my head.
But I've no spade to follow men like them.

Between my finger and my thumb
The squat pen rests.
I'll dig with it.

2 *squat* [skwɒt] (adj.): short and thick • *snug:* warm and comfortable **6** *strain* (v.): make the greatest possible effort • *rump* (infml.): person's bottom **8** *drill:* Furche **10** *nestle* ['nesl]: settle comfortably • *lug:* projecting part of an object by which it may be carried **11** *lever* ['li:və ☆ 'levər] (v.): hebeln **17** *turf* [tɜ:f ☆ tɜ:rf] (U): (in Irland) Torf **18** *Toner's bog:* moor in Co. Londonderry **20** *sloppy* (adj.): careless **21** *fall to:* begin **22** *nick sth.:* make a small cut in sth. • *heave sb./sth.* (v.): lift sb./sth. with great effort • *sod:* piece of turf (cf. l. 17) **25** *mould* (BE) = (AE) *mold:* Schimmelpilz, Moder • *squelch* [skweltʃ] (n.): Platschen **26** *soggy:* very wet • *peat* (U): Torf • *curt:* short; abrupt

Seamus Heaney

Chapter V

The Time Ahead

1

Canon Samuel H. Reid

The Irish Problem

The following text takes a look at the history of Ireland and the Irish and draws conclusions for the future.

When the Irish Problem is mentioned the immediate response is to say that it has been caused by the partition of Ireland in 1921, and the solution is simply that "the British" should leave. This ignores the fact that a substantial majority of people in the North of Ireland still count themselves as British (as well as Irish) and would like the situation to remain as it is.

The slogan "Ireland for the Irish" prompts the question "Who *are* the Irish?" One answer would be to say that they are the original inhabitants of the country. When we apply this test, history reveals that the first inhabitants were not the Celts, often spoken of as the true ancestors of the Irish, but the Picts who came across the narrow North Channel from Scotland. Indeed the "first" inhabitants are generally believed to have entered the country at Larne. Ever since there have been many comings and goings between Ireland, especially the North of Ireland, and Scotland, and there is much affinity between the two countries. Even today the speech of a person from Ballymena could easily be taken for that of an inhabitant of Scotland.

Ireland, like most other countries, experienced many invasions. We have already mentioned the Picts and then the Celts. These were followed over the centuries by the Danes, the Normans, the English, and perhaps one should add the Huguenots from France. We may as well ask how long a person must be living in a country before he or she is accepted as a citizen? Really the quest for the "pure" Irish is a fruitless one. We are all a mixture!

Partition or division is not just a modern Irish problem. There have been divisions since ancient times – even between north and south! One can point to a structure known as the Black Pig's Dyke. Extensive remains of this earthen fortification still exist, running across Ireland from Carlingford Lough, near Newry in the East, to the Atlantic Ocean near Bundoran in the West. Ancient Ireland was also divided into four provinces, each with a king, and a fifth province with the High King, who ruled at Tara.

But enough of history! The present position is that the island of Ireland is made up of two communities opposed to each other in many important ways. Religion is not the only ingredient, but the divisions which spring from the 16th century Reformation have made a difficult problem even more difficult.

But what about a solution? Many people have tried and failed, so the outlook is bleak.

A possible way out might be for the two states – north and south – to establish a truly pluralist country, where people of different races and religions would find it possible to work together for the good of all.

One of the fears of the Northern Protestants is that the Roman Catholic Church exerts too much influence in the South and that this would be reflected in a so-called "United" Ireland. In spite of the charges of bigotry in the North, a community is developing where freedom for all is being practised.

It is difficult to visualize a coming-together of the two parts of Ireland, at least in the foreseeable future.

Why not make it possible for each part to remain as it is, practising good neighbourliness to the other part, with a Bill of Rights to guarantee the rights of minorities. There should be no talk about coercion or force so that the healing qualities of years, if not centuries, would make it possible to establish closer, friendlier links throughout Ireland.

Canon: Protestant priest with special duties in a cathedral **2** *partition of Ireland in 1921:* cf. "Info-Box", p. 21 **3** *substantial:* considerable **11** *Larne:* seaport near Belfast **17** *Huguenot* ['hjuːgənəʊ]: (formerly) French Protestant **19** *quest* (fml.): search **23** *dyke:* long wall of earth **31** *bleak* (fig.): not hopeful; gloomy **43** *coercion* [kəʊ'ɜːʃn ☆ -'ɜːrʃn] (U): use of force or threats to make sb. do sth.

A peaceful future for Northern Ireland – illusion or reality? (Scene in Belfast's city centre)

2

Joe Rogaly

The Pieces of the Puzzle

In the following article from the *Financial Times* a journalist examines three possible solutions to the problems of Northern Ireland, showing the effects that each might have.

There is no short-term solution to the problem of Northern Ireland. There just may be a long-term one, if the British Prime Minister takes it seriously enough. This is plain if you re-examine the pieces of the puzzle, as most of us outside the unhappy province have to do each time there is a resurgence in violence terrible enough to focus our constantly wandering attention upon it. The awful scenes on our television screens last week, particularly those in which two young British soldiers were murdered by a bloodthirsty mob, have been exceptionally shocking, and have thus had an exceptional effect upon the British consciousness. Let us, therefore, look again for a road to peace.

In Britain, three possibilities have been widely discussed by politicians and the saloon-bar public alike over the past few weeks. The first is the withdrawal of the British Army from Northern Ireland, with only a sour curse on both sides as a parting gift. The second is the very reverse: an intensification of the campaign against paramilitary organisations in both communities, aided by such devices as internment, the re-introduction of capital punishment and the determined use of killer commandos such as the SAS. The third is to persist with efforts to defeat the IRA and its Protestant counterparts, while working with the Irish Government as the significance of the border between north and south is eroded. Call these options "troops out", "troops in", and "containment-plus".

We can dismiss the first quite quickly. Some isolated Labour politicians and a great many on the extreme left of British politics support "troops out", but the idea does not stand up to examination. It suffers from the initial (and to me overriding) disadvantage that it would constitute a vindication of the IRA strategy of terrorist violence – but, even for those who could swallow that, it has a further, fatal flaw. It would not end the violence, but intensify it. On this matter there is a chilling near-unanimity among British politicians with a close acquaintance with Northern Ireland.

What they say is that, in the absence of a British military force, the Protestant paramilitary organisations would seek to restore the Unionist ascendancy. There would be political murders and virtual civil war. The locally recruited police and defence forces, which have been built up as means of reducing the front-line activities of the British Army, would doubtless involve themselves.

The minority Catholic population could not win such a battle on its own. It would be almost impossible for any Dublin Government to restrain itself from going to the Catholics' assistance. Cooperation between Washington and London on security would be under severe strain;one consequence might be that "volunteers" from the Irish community in the US would come over to join the fray. (If you have ever sat through a night's patriotic singing in one of New York's Irish bars you will find this easy to believe.) As one British minister said this week, "you would have the Spanish civil war replayed on our doorstep." Some people doubt that the loyalists would start such an affray, but the risk is not worth contemplating.

So what, then, about "troops in"? This would attract strong support from many people in Britain, not least those on the Conservative back benches who have been muttering all week about the desirability of "going in there and sorting them out." But this, too, would not work. The last time internment was introduced, in 1971, violence increased sharply. There was an international outcry. Support for the IRA was probably strengthened. Again, capital punishment would produce martyrs, upon which organisations like the IRA thrive. Some of the Tories who support capital punishment in general have been heard to say, "but of course not in Northern Ireland."

It may be objected, particularly in saloon-bar conversations, that this is all

INFO BOX

The Anglo-Irish Agreement

In November 1985 an agreement was signed by the governments of the United Kingdom and the Republic of Ireland. The fundamental objectives of this agreement were to promote peace and stability in Northern Ireland, to establish equal rights for the two sections of the community and to achieve a reconciliation between them. For this purpose, an intergovernmental conference was established, allowing the Irish Government to put forward views and proposals on matters concerning Northern Ireland. The United Kingdom saw the agreement as a means of getting the two governments to combine forces not only to defeat terrorism but also to bring about a political process which would eventually end the conflict between nationalists and Unionists in Northern Ireland.

Under the terms of the agreement there was to be more cooperation between security forces on both sides of the border dividing Northern and Southern Ireland. For example, a programme of work was to be drawn up by top policemen on either side, dealing with such topics as the exchange of information, technical cooperation and the training of personnel.

Although the British and Irish Governments are committed to seeking devolution, i.e. limited self-government, involving both communities in the administration of Northern Ireland, it was specifically stated in the agreement that there would be no change in the status of the province without the consent of a majority of its people.

This last statement was meant by the UK government as a guarantee to the Ulster Unionists. These, however, have reacted very strongly against the agreement and still refuse to accept it. They feel betrayed since they were not consulted beforehand, and they object to the fact that a foreign government, i.e. the Irish Government in Dublin, has been given a significant role in Northern Ireland's internal affairs. The fact that the Irish Government has, in some cases, refused to send people accused of terrorist activities to Northern Ireland for trial has further angered the Unionists.

Since the implementation of the agreement there have been improvements in cross-border cooperation concerning security, but political reconciliation between the two traditions has not come about so far.

The Rev. Ian Paisley, one of the most vehement opponents of the Anglo-Irish Agreement

very well but that if the British forces were unleashed they could wipe out the men of violence. People who take this view express little disquiet at allegations that there was a "shoot-to-kill" policy at the start of the decade, or that something very like such a policy was in use in Gibraltar when the three terrorists who were buried last week were shot in the street by the SAS. The trouble with this line of thinking is that we live in a democracy. One important difference between the IRA and the British Government is that the latter stands for the rule of law. In our society, assassinations of doubtful legality raise more questions than they answer. They breed further hostility against the British. Seriously "wiping out" an enemy requires the callousness of a Stalin, a Hitler, or a Pol Pot.

We are therefore left with the third option, which is "containment-plus". The recent series of awful events may lead some people to think that the containment side of this policy is not working. In fact [...] the number of violent deaths has been brought under a sort of control over the past decade. The sharp increase in the number of people injured over the past couple of years, and the increase in civilian deaths last year, is ascribed by Unionists to the Anglo-Irish Agreement, which was signed in November, 1985. I will come to that agreement in a moment, but first it should be recognised that a great deal of the killing and counter-killing has taken place between the security forces and their insurgent opponents, or between paramilitary factions. The Provisional IRA contains some of the most sophisticated terrorists in western Europe; increasingly they have been matched, and outmatched, by British intelligence. Examples of the result were seen in May 1987, when eight IRA men, and a passing motorist, were killed in an ambush at Loughgall police station – and, again, in Gibraltar the other day.

The plus side of "containment-plus" is the Anglo-Irish Agreement, which is as important for its psychological impact as for what it says. It acknowledges the existence of international concern for the affairs of the province first because it has been registered at the United Nations and, second, because it provides for continual consultation with the Republic of Ireland. Britain retains sovereignty, but it cannot be said to be undiluted.

To some British politicians the long-term purpose of the agreement is to prepare for the day when the people of Northern Ireland have been persuaded to vote for a transfer of sovereignty from London to Dublin. This is not the view of the Prime Minister or of her several Secretaries of State for Northern Ireland. The Ulster Protestants may be exasperating, but the Conservatives would not accept a strategy of selling them down the Liffey.

The purposes of the agreement are, first, to remove the sting of international pressure and, second, to persuade the Protestant community that it must come to some kind of political understanding with the Catholics if its future is to be secure. The first purpose has been met. President Reagan has recognised the significance of the agreement, as has the European Community. It could also be argued that the issue of the border has been defused. Its significance will be further eroded in 1992, when the EC abolishes internal customs posts and establishes a single economic regime. The Irish Government for its part has had to accept responsibilities.

As to the second purpose, a forthcoming book, *Northern Ireland since 1968* by Paul Arthur and Keith Jeffery (Basil Blackwell/Institute of Contemporary British History) suggests that progress is being made. "The loyalists," say the authors, "are still out in the cold and, indeed, are in some disarray. But there appears to be a slow Unionist realisation that old methods and old cliches are no longer relevant. In short, the Anglo-Irish Agreement has at least made that psychological breakthrough." We can already see results. For example, the contribution of the formerly fiery Unionist Mr Peter Robinson to Monday afternoon's debate in the House of Commons was noteworthy for its tone of moderation.

It is plainly necessary for the British Government to tread with great delicacy on these new-laid eggs. Lean too hard towards Dublin, and the old Protestant fears of a "United Ireland" are rekindled. Allow too many events that seem like anti-Catholic outrages to pile up, and the local pressure on the Irish Government to dilute the significance of the agreement is intensified. For this reason, the ministers and permanent secretaries at the Foreign Office, the Home Office, the Northern Ireland Office, Defence and Treasury have been persuaded, over the past few weeks, of the desirability of introducing an "Irish dimension" into the review of new Government policies. There is just such an international understanding in Whitehall over the "European dimension" – how will this play in Brussels? Now a new question has been added: "How will it play in Dublin and Belfast?"

8 *resurgence* [rɪ'sɜːdʒəns ☆ -'sɜːr-] (U) (fml.): rise; revival **12–13** *two young British soldiers were murdered:* reference to the killing of two British undercover agents on March 19, 1988, who were observing the funeral of an IRA member killed by an Protestant gunman **27–28** *internment* (U): imprisonment without trial **30** *SAS* (abbr.) = *Special Air Service:* unit of the British Army specially trained to fight terrorists **31** *persist with sth. :* continue doing sth. **35** *erode sth.:* destroy sth. gradually **37** *containment* (U): keeping sth. within limits, so that it cannot spread harmfully **38** *dismiss sb./sth.:* consider sb./sth. not worth thinking or talking about **43–44** *overriding* (adj.): more important than any other considerations **45** *vindication* (U) (fml.): Rechtfertigung **48** *flaw:* fault; weakness

49–50 *chilling* (adj.): frightening • *near-unanimity* (U): nearly com-plete agreement **56** *ascendancy* [ə'sendənsɪ ☆ -si:] (U): (position of) having dominant power or control **57** *virtual* ['vɜ:tʃʊəl ☆ 'vɜ:r-]: faktisch **72** *fray* (fml.): fight **80** *affray* [– '–] (fml.): disturbance of the peace caused by fighting or rioting **85** *back bench:* (in Britain) seat in the House of Commons for an MP who does not hold an important position in the government or opposition **87–88** *sort sb. out* (sl.): deal with sb. by punishing or attacking them **95** *Tory:* (in Britain) member of the Conservative Party **102** *unleash sth.* (fig.): set sth. free from control **104** *allegation:* statement made without proof **107** *Gibraltar:* reference to the killing of three unarmed IRA members by the SAS (cf. l. 30) on March 6, 1988; it was claimed that the guerrillas had planted a car bomb **119** *callousness:* cruelly insensitive behaviour **119–120** *Pol Pot* (1926–): Kampuchean politician; dictatorial prime minister 1976–1979 **132** *ascribe sth. to sb./sth.:* consider sth. to be caused by sb./sth. **132–133** *Anglo-Irish Agreement:* cf. "Info-Box", p. 67 **139** *insurgent* [ɪn'sɜ:dʒənt ☆ -'sɜ:r-]: rebellious **144** *intelligence* (U): people gathering information of military value **148** *Loughgall* [lɒx'gɔ:l] **160** *undiluted* [ˌʌndaɪ'lju:tɪd ☆ -'lu:-] (adj.) (fig.): undiminished in force or effect **172** *Liffey* ['lɪfɪ]: river flowing through Dublin **184** *defuse sth.* (fig.): reduce the dangerous tension in sth. **197** *disarray* [– – '–] (U): disorganization **210** *tread* [tred] (v.): walk or step **213** *rekindle sth.* [ˌri:'kɪndl]: cause sth. to light again **226** *Whitehall:* the British Government **228** *play* (v.): (here) be regarded

Talking about the text

1. Name the three policies that, according to the writer, are being discussed in Britain with regard to Northern Ireland.
2. What are the writer's main reasons for rejecting a withdrawal of the British Army from Northern Ireland?
3. In what respect would Britain's foreign relations be put under strain by withdrawing all troops from Northern Ireland?
4. Outline the writer's reasons for rejecting the idea of drastically intensifying the fight against terrorism in Northern Ireland.
5. Weigh up Joe Rogaly's arguments for and against the third possibility of dealing with the situation.
6. In what ways, according to Joe Rogaly, does the Anglo-Irish Agreement point to hope for the future?

3

BILLY SIMPSON
17 Years Later

17 years after the *Belfast Telegraph* organized an essay competition for schoolchildren, the newspaper looked again at some of the entries and revisited the winner.

In the summer of 1970 this newspaper ran an essay competition which invited school-children to write about "The Kind of Ulster I Want." Over 400 children submitted essays. One of the judges of the competition wrote at the time: "We did not expect many of the entries to be constructive. Nor did we expect them to produce such a painful indictment of the sickness in our society."

The excerpts from the essays that came from children and teenagers were published over a number of weeks and many displayed a maturity and perception that sometimes astonished and sometimes amused.

Here are a few examples ...

"An ideal Ulster would be where adults don't act like children, and disagreements don't lead to fighting." – *Girl, aged 11, Belfast.*

"I would like Ulster to be a place where sectarianism, bigotry and discrimination are only big words in a dictionary. It is a pity that Ulster with all its beauty is bleeding itself to death." – *Boy, aged 13, Derry.*

"I would hate Ulster to be goody-goody as I don't think anywhere in the world is perfect, but shooting people dead in the street is too much." – *Girl, aged 12, Belfast.*

"If all Ulster has left are Paisleyite bigots or Irish Nationalist fanatics then for a start off, this essay is ridiculous as there will soon be no Ulster left to want anything for." – *Girl, aged 15, Strabane.*

"An Ulster united with Eire, where all denominations are allowed to practise their religions without discrimination." – *Boy, aged 11, Londonderry.*

"My Ulster would keep Southern Ireland separate by means of a giant canal or wide waterway right along the border. This would not only separate the two countries but provide work for all the unemployed people of Belfast, Strabane, Newry and Armagh." – *Boy, aged 11, Larne.*

"Ulster's illness is not so much physical as mental. Ulster's prime need is not a physician but a psychiatrist." – *Boy, aged 15, Belfast.*

"I would like to see the end of the Qualifying exam even though I passed it. It isn't really fair because the girl who was first in my class didn't pass it." – *Girl, aged 12, Richill.*

"I want an Ulster without any fighting, none at all." – *Girl, aged 9, Hillsborough.*

Most of the children who took part in the competition all those years ago are now in their late 20s or early 30s.

We decided to contact a couple of the winners to give them a chance to read their winning essays again and tell us if they still believed in the same high ideals they wrote about 17 years ago.

The overall winning essay in 1970 was written by a 14-year-old pupil at Wallace High School in Lisburn, John Ross, who at that time lived in Killeaton Park, Dunmurry. [...]

John Ross's prize winning essay of 1970 is published below and we talk to him about his life and views today.

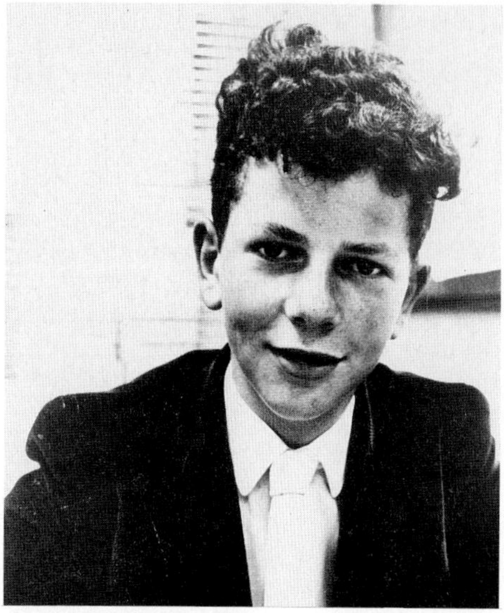

Here's what John Ross said in 1970

When my studies have ended I would like to go abroad for a few years to Canada, Australia or New Zealand.

On my arrival in one of these distant lands someone is sure to ask: "What part of the world do you come from?" In answer to that question I hope and pray I will be proud to say "from Northern Ireland".

A lot will have to be done between now and then if my hopes are to be fulfilled. A new Ulster must be built, an Ulster in which trust has replaced suspicion and understanding has taken the place of hatred.

"Live and let live" must become the motto of our province and it must never be forgotten. People of all faiths must learn to live side by side and work together in peace for the good of all.

The kind of Ulster I want must be the kind of Ulster everyone who loves this little corner of Ireland wants. I believe we can be given it by a good, honest government backed by a progressive people who look to the future and give little thought to the past.

We have been living too much in the past and thinking too little of the future. But it is the future that counts. The past is sad. Let us make the future happier so that years from now when we look back the memories will be happy ones.

The Ulster I want will have work for all who want it and plenty of facilities for spending leisure happily and at little cost. All slum dwellings will be demolished and new homes provided for all who need them at rents they can afford.

All homes, even country cottages, will have a bathroom and running water. There will be no waiting lists for houses and as a result there will be less unhappiness and discontent.

In the Ulster I want children of all faiths would attend the same schools. If this is impossible then I would like to see pupils of Roman Catholic and Protestant schools brought together as often as possible for sports and games and week-end camps.

A Roman Catholic school could adopt a Protestant school and vice versa for these purposes. I am sure these meetings would go a long way to ensuring peace in the future.

I would like to see a swimming pool, a proper playground and a community centre provided in every town in Ulster, and I would like to see more schemes to help Ulster school children travel and see something of the world outside Northern Ireland, at little cost to their parents.

In the Ulster I want the countryside would be free of horrible piles of litter, which are nearly everywhere now – old cars, bedsteads, mattresses and rusty tins. With the litter must go the offensive slogans on walls. The new Ulster must be fresh.

When the kind of Ulster I want is built it will be the sort of place to which I can invite my pen pals from France and Germany and be proud to show them. It will be the sort of place that will so impress the visitor that he will say on leaving: "I can hardly wait till I come back."

And what John Ross says today

When he was a 14-year-old schoolboy at Wallace High School, John Ross had plans to study medicine and later emigrate to Canada, Australia or New Zealand.

"Life seldom works out as you imagine it when you are young," says John, now a 31-year-old schoolteacher, living in Craigavon. "But I am thoroughly happy the way things are."

Married with two young sons, he has no regrets about staying in Northern Ireland. "There are times when I look at the kids and wonder whether this is really the place to be bringing them up. On the other hand, other countries have their problems too," he said. "I am not pessimistic. In fact at the moment I am fairly optimistic about the way things are beginning to go. There seems to be some sense coming into the situation. It had to come sometime."

The main theme of his prize winning essay (reprinted on this page) was a plea to "Live and let live". It is an ideal he still believes in strongly.

His decision to become a schoolteacher was made when he was studying history at the Ulster University at Coleraine in the 70s. "I never thought of teaching until my middle years at University. Maybe it had something to do with meeting so many teachers up there."

While he was at university, he and some other students travelled around Europe – France, Spain, Italy, Switzerland, Yugoslavia and Greece. But it was Europe on a shoe-string. "We slept on beaches and in disused cinemas," he said.

It was at Coleraine where he met his wife, Eileen, who was also a student. They lived in Portstewart during her final year at university. He graduated a year earlier.

Eileen now works in the civil service.

After qualifying as a teacher, John worked as a substitute teacher in a number of schools, both Catholic and State. In 1980 he joined the teaching staff of Deramore High School, Belfast, where he still teaches.

Re-reading the schoolboy essay after 17 years, he felt some of the things he wanted to see happen in Ulster were at last happening.

"We have come a long way since then," he said. "In 1970 integrated education was not talked about much. Now there are four or five integrated schools in the province. I think integrated education is important. I think this is where we have to start. With the kids. Even by the time they reach secondary school, it is too late. We need integrated primary education."

He feels that in many ways schools are better than they were 17 years ago. "The educational standards remain much the same but there is a different atmosphere now. More open. Freer. Teacher-pupil relationships are better than in my day. Teachers are not held in the same awe. Possibly we have lost some of the respect but I think teachers are more approachable nowadays.

"Having gone into teaching I find that I enjoy it. It has its ups and downs but it is very rewarding.

"I like living in Craigavon. It is very quiet. Semi-rural. Good facilities. I enjoy fishing and Lough Mask is just two miles down the road, and there are the balancing lakes. What destroyed Craigavon was not having a major industry."

His 17-year-old essay, viewed from an adult perspective, was "very idealistic" he said. "When you get into your 20s and start bringing up a family, looking for a job and paying a mortgage, you think less about where the country is going. But basically I am an optimist. I am hopeful for the future. You have to be to live in this country. It is a beautiful province. If you got the weather you couldn't beat it."

9 *indictment* [ɪn'daɪtmənt] (fig.): accusation **23** *sectarianism* (U) (derog.): quality of showing a lack of tolerance or concern for those outside one's own sect, class, etc. • *bigotry* ['bɪgətrɪ ☆ -triː] (U): intolerance, narrow-mindedness **28** *goody-goody* (adj.) (derog.): be-having so as to appear very virtuous and respectable **33** *Paisleyite* ['peɪzlɪaɪt] (adj.): of or belonging to a follower of Ian Paisley (1926–), a Northern Irish Protestant clergyman and strong adversary of Catholicism • *bigot* ['bɪgət]: intolerant and narrow-minded person **37** *Strabane* [strə'bæn] **38** *Eire* ['eərə] (Irish): Republic of Ireland **54** *Qualifying exam:* (in Northern Ireland) examination taken by children at the age of 11 to decide whether they may go to grammar school **112** *dwelling* (fml.): house; flat **130** *go a long way to doing sth.:* help greatly in achieving sth. **160–161** *Craigavon* [kreɪg'ævən] **176** *plea* (fml.): earnest request **189–190** *on a shoe-string* (infml.): using very little money **209** *integrated education* (U): school system in which students belonging to different racial or religious groups are taught together (cf. "Info-Box", p. 75) **223** *hold sb./sth. in awe:* respect sb./sth. very much **233–234** *balancing lakes:* small lakes on the southern shore of Lough Neagh [ˌlɒx neɪ] **240** *mortgage* ['mɔːgɪdʒ ☆ 'mɔːr-]: sum of money borrowed from a bank to buy a house

Youths in the Skankill area of Belfast collecting wood for the yearly bonfire in celebration of the Protestant victory at the Battle of the Boyne in 1690

Bridging the divide – Protestant and Catholic pupils at Lagan College, Northern Ireland's first integrated school

INFO BOX

Integrated Education

In the Northern Irish education system there has always been a clear separation in both primary and secondary sectors between Catholics and Protestants, with Protestant children being educated in state schools and most Catholic children attending Roman Catholic maintained schools.

In 1974 a body called "All Children Together" was set up by a group of parents with the aim of supporting education in schools acceptable to all religious affiliations and cultural traditions. In 1981 Lagan College, the first integrated school in Northern Ireland, was opened in Belfast, and there are now 10 integrated schools in all, both primary and secondary, with several more in the planning stages. These schools are scattered all over the country, and they try to achieve an even balance of Catholics and Protestants among pupils, staff and management. The curriculum reflects the two traditions in Northern Ireland, and the British and Irish cultures are present in subjects such as History, Religious Education, Music, Art, Sports and Literature. The Irish language is offered as a subject at all integrated schools, and both British games, such as hockey and rugby, and Irish games, such as camogie and hurling, are played.

Under the conditions of the Education Reform Act of February 1990, the government will for now meet the cost of teachers' salaries and will pay a proportion of the running costs of new integrated schools. However, these schools will still have to find voluntary funding to meet all other costs. The passing of this new act is due in no small measure to parental pressure through "All Children Together", and it demonstrates a slow but steady growing together of the two communities.

4

Carmel McQuaid

Starting with the Young

Most observers are agreed that children and young people play a key role in the future development of Northern Ireland. What does not seem so clear, though, is whether children should be seen more as part of the problem or part of the solution.

a) Disobey Parents, Ulster Pupils Urged

If schools in Northern Ireland could persuade pupils to rebel against their parents and community, the civil conflict would end, a psychology lecturer has advised.

In his book, *Caught in Crossfire: Children and the Northern Ireland Conflict*, Dr Ed Cairns, of the University of Ulster, says that the obedient nature of Ulster's youngsters is perpetuating the religious divide.

The young people attend church and school regularly, give their teachers little trouble, and keep on the right side of the law.

Dr Cairns warned: "The violence of the 1970s and 1980s could furnish the script for political behaviour over the next 50 years. If one day the two communities are to live in harmony, something will have to be done to ensure that Northern Ireland does not continue to produce children who tend towards conformity with their parents."

The scene of the 1987 Enniskillen bombing as the coffin of one of the victims is carried past

The book cites a survey which raises more fears: 2,785 children from Northern Ireland, the Irish Republic, Jordan and Iraq were asked to write for 10 minutes on "My Country". The Ulster sample mentioned politics less frequently and violence more often than the others. "This political apathy carried into adulthood could leave the way open for violence to dominate in the years to come," he stated.

Sectarian attitudes also emerged when 120 Catholic and Protestant boys, aged from six to nine, were asked to sort orange, green, red and blue geometric figures. They were immediately alert to the political-religious symbolism of the colours.

Suggestions that red and blue (the Union Jack) be grouped with green (the Irish flag) were rejected by the older children who exclaimed: "No that's not right; you can't put Protestants with Catholics." The same experiment, conducted among Scottish children, found colours did not matter.

Neither sector, however, displays the psychological traits associated with minorities. While 50 per cent of Ulster pupils can detect religion from Christian names at seven and 70 per cent at 11, few can do so at a younger age – unlike children in racially dominated societies who start to categorize socially at five.

Ulster pupils also differ from minorities in that they rarely misidentify their own group. "The problem is best thought of as involving two psychological majorities," Dr Cairns concludes.

The author warns that the desire to conserve schools as "havens of peace" can only inhibit the open inter-group discussion vital for reconciliation. Schools, he argues, could provide the ideal scenario for examining such aspects of the conflict as feature in history and social science. Equipped with background knowledge, pupils could then continue the theme with a group from the opposite school system.

"The syndrome where the existence of the conflict is denied is undoubtedly a major obstacle to peace," Dr Cairns concludes.

---

b) A Field Where Hope Grows

Two catastrophes of the Ulster troubles – the 1987 Poppy Day Massacre and the 1979 Mountbatten boat bombing – have fired a determined attempt to set up an integrated school in Enniskillen.

The Fermanagh Integrated School Project is being led by a 52-year-old teacher, Mr John Maxwell, whose son Paul, 17, died with Lord Mountbatten and two others when their boat was bombed at Mullaghmore, Co. Sligo.

It was the atmosphere of goodwill between the communities in the aftermath of the 1987 cenotaph bombing which finally prompted the launch of his plan. A series of meetings, advertised by word of mouth, enlisted several other supporters and their first formal gathering drew an audience of 200.

The project has been hampered by the fact that the new legislation which will give cash aid to integrated schools has not yet become law. Fund-raising activities, such as crèches for Christmas shoppers, have therefore had to be organized.

But a suitable location for the school has now been found in a 12-acre greenfield site at Drumcoo. Initially, only three acres are being bought and lessons will have to start in a mobile classroom. A teacher is, however, being recruited and 45 children are due to enrol in September.

With roughly equal numbers of Catholics and Protestants in the area, the project's organizers are confident they can achieve a good religious mix. John Maxwell, however, shakes off extravagant claims for the project as a solution to all the community's ills. He sees it as merely one way for the process of coming together to begin.

A sociology teacher at the local FE college, he cites research evidence that daily, face-to-face contact and a common goal can defuse antagonism. He has personally seen how Catholic and Protestant students, having sometimes on their first day in FE congregated on opposite sides of the room, begin slowly to mix after a few weeks – becoming good friends by the end of the year. "I am absolutely convinced of the value of integrated education. Contact has to be ongoing to be effective."

The project, while a team effort, has been a lifeline for John Maxwell, who has suffered from depression since Paul's death. During the last few months he has ceased to be wakened by nightmares and he hopes that by September 1, 1989, the trauma of his loss will have eased further.

"Involvement with this project has meant that increasingly I feel I am living rather than going through the motions. The morning Enniskillen opens its integrated school will be a big day in my life. My loss shall have yielded something positive."

19 *furnish sth.:* provide sth. **38** *sectarian* (derog.): showing a lack of tolerance or concern for those outside one's own sect, class, etc. • *emerge:* become known **54** *trait:* element in sb.'s personality **67** *haven* ['heɪvn]: place of safety or rest **68** *inhibit sth.:* hinder or prevent sth. **69** *vital* ['vaɪtl]: essential • *reconciliation* (U): Versöhnung **72** *feature* (v.): have an important part **83** *Poppy Day* (infml.): (in Britain) Remembrance Sunday, the Sunday nearest to the 11th November, when the dead of both world wars are remembered; (here) day in 1987 when a bomb exploded in Enniskillen, killing 11 people **84** *Mountbatten = Lord Louis Mountbatten* (1900–1979): British admiral, killed when his boat was blown up off the west coast of Ireland **86** *integrated school:* school in which students belonging to different racial or religious groups are taught together (cf. "Info-Box", p. 75) • *Enniskillen:* town in Co. Fermanagh **92** *Sligo* ['slaɪgəʊ] **94** *aftermath:* circumstances that follow and are the consequences of an event (esp. an unpleasant one) **95** *cenotaph* ['senətɑːf ☆ -tæf]: monument in memory of people buried elsewhere, esp. soldiers killed in war; (here) site of the 1987 Enniskillen bomb explosion (cf. l. 83) **96** *prompt sth.:* cause sth. • *launch* [lɔːntʃ] (n.) (fig.): process of putting sth. into motion **98** *enlist sb.* [– '–]: get the support of sb. **101** *hamper sb./sth.:* hinder sb./sth. **105** *crèche* [kreʃ] (BE): nursery where babies are looked after **108** *site:* place where a building will be situated **113** *enrol* (BE) = (AE) *enroll* [ɪn'rəʊl]: become a member **123** *FE* (abbr.) = *Further Education:* formal (but not university) education provided for people older than school age **124** *cite sb./sth.:* quote sb./sth. **126** *defuse sth.* (fig.): reduce the dangerous tension in sth. • *antagonism* [– '– – –]: feeling of hate **137** *lifeline* (fig.): anything on which sb./sth. depends for continued existence **146** *go through the motions* (infml.): pretend to do sth.; do sth. without sincerity **149** *yield sth.* [jiːld]: produce sth.

Talking about the text

1. Explain the statement cited in ll. 3–6.
2. What is the significance of the colour test described in ll. 38–52?
3. Sum up the background to the integrated school project in Enniskillen.
4. Compare the roles Ed Cairns and John Maxwell assign to schools in the effort to end violence in Northern Ireland.

Acknowledgments

Texts

I/1 "An Untamed Land So Far from Trouble" by Cal McCrystal from *The Sunday Times* of 31 May, 1987. © Times Newspapers Limited 1987.

I/2 From *An Ulster Journey* by Alf McCreary, Greystone Press, 1986. Reprinted by permission of W & G Baird Limited, Antrim.

I/3 From *A Place Apart* by Dervla Murphy. Reprinted by permission of John Murray (Publishers) Ltd.

II/1 "Twenty Years on, 'When Will It Ever End?'" by Edmund Curran and Frederick Painton from *Time* of 22 August, 1988. Copyright 1988 Time Inc. Reprinted by permission.

II/2 From *Tried by Fire: Finding Hope out of Suffering in Northern Ireland* by Alf McCreary, Marshall Pickering, 1986. Reprinted by permission of Marshall Pickering.

II/3a From the *Daily Mirror* of 10 August, 1989. Reprinted by permission.

II/3b From *Today* (Ulster edition) of 11 August, 1989. Reproduced by kind permission of *Today*.

II/4 From *To Stay Alive* by Linda Anderson. Copyright © Linda Anderson 1984. Published by The Bodley Head & Futura. Reprinted by permission.

II/5 "Enemy Encounter" by Padraic Fiacc from Frank Ormsby (ed.), *Poets from the North of Ireland,* The Blackstaff Press, 1979. Reprinted by permission.

III/1 "Life Goes On in 'Neutral Zone'" by Frank Davies from *News Letter* of 9 August, 1986. Reprinted by permission of CN Century Newspapers Ltd.

III/2 "Claudy" by James Simmons from *Poems 1956–1986* (1986) by kind permission of the author and The Gallery Press, Loughcrew, Oldcastle, Co. Meath, Ireland.

III/3 From *See Me, See Her* by John Pepper, The Blackstaff Press, 1978. Reprinted by permission.

III/4 From *Images of Belfast* by Robert Johnstone and Bill Kirk, Blackstaff Press, 1983. Reprinted by permission.

IV/1 "Once Alien Here" by John Hewitt from Frank Ormsby (ed.), *Poets from the North of Ireland,* The Blackstaff Press, 1979. Reprinted by permission.

IV/2 "Father and Son" by Bernard MacLaverty from *Scottish Short Stories*, Collins, 1978. Reprinted by permission.

IV/3 From "The Ulster Renaissance" by Donna Foote and David Lehman from *Newsweek* of 12 May 1986, Newsweek, Inc. All rights reserved. Reprinted by permission.

IV/4 From *Ourselves Alone* by Anne Devlin. Reprinted by permission of Faber and Faber Ltd.

IV/5 From *Death of a Naturalist* by Seamus Heaney. Reprinted by permission of Faber and Faber Ltd.

V/1 "The Irish Problem" by Canon Samuel H. Reid printed by permission.

V/2 From "What Britain Can Do about Ireland" by Joe Rogaly from the *Financial Times* of 25 March, 1988. Reprinted by permission of Financial Times Syndication.

V/3 From "Seventeen Years on, Is This the Kind of Ulster They Wanted?" by Billy Simpson from the *Belfast Telegraph* of 26 August, 1987. Reprinted by permission.

V/4a "Disobey Parents, Ulster Pupils Urged" by Carmel McQuaid from *The Times Educational Supplement* of 14 August, 1987. © Times Newspapers Limited 1987.

V/4b "A Field Where Hope Grows" by Carmel McQuaid from *The Times Educational Supplement* of 6 January, 1989. © Times Newspapers Limited 1989.

Illustrations

Belfast Telegraph: pp. 27, 72, 73; Gabriele Heinisch, Berlin, © Cornelsen Verlag, Berlin, 1990: pp. 9, 14, 44; Northern Ireland Tourist Board: pp. 6, 8, 12, 16, 38, 41, 50, 65; Pacemaker Press International Ltd.: pp. 19, 21, 25, 32, 49, 63, 68, 74, 75, 76; Punch: p. 46; Christian v. Raumer, Berlin, p. 43; Uwe Tröger, Berlin: p. 59; Writers and Readers Publishing Cooperative Society Ltd.: p. 33.